Too Much Water
Too Much Rain

The Story of The Alstead Flood

Alstead Historical Society

Edited by
Cassandra Kreek
Emily K. Kreek
Ian D. Relihan

PublishingWorks
Exeter, NH
2006

Copyright © 2006. Alstead Historical Society, Inc. All rights reserved.

Printed in Canada.

First Printing.

Published by:

PublishingWorks, Inc.
60 Winter Street
Exeter, NH 03833
603-778-9883

Ordering:

Revolution Booksellers, LLC
60 Winter Street
Exeter, NH 03833
603-772-7200
1-800-REV-6603

www.revolutionbooksellers.com

LCCN: 2006931176

ISBN: 1-933002-38-7
ISBN: 13-978-1-933002-38-7

DEDICATION

This book is dedicated to the memory of those who lost their lives in the Alstead Flood of 2005:

> *Sally Canfield*
> *Timothy Canfield*
> *Spencer Petty*
> *William Seale*

And in grateful thanks to the thousands of "neighbors" who shared their time, possessions, and resources in time of need to help make Alstead whole again.

View of Forest Road (Route 123). *Oil painting by Heidi Hernes*

Alstead Village Bridge after the flood, October 2005. *Oil painting by Heidi Hernes*

Contents

Preface vi
The Waters **1**
    Alstead 2
    Cold River 10
    Warren Brook 12
    Storm Brewing 18
Floodwatch **21**
    Friday 22
    Saturday 22
    Sunday Morning 31
The Flood **41**
Overcoming Chaos **79**
    Neighbor Helping Neighbor 80
    Search for the Missing 97
    Loss 98
    Town Meeting 110
The Town Recovers **111**
    The Animals 112
    The Children 114
    Everyday Inconveniences 122
Rebuilding **127**
    Where to Start? 129
    The Work 130
    Around the Clock 133
    As It Is 137
    Why? 138
    States of Mind 139
Alstead Today **143**
    The Future 148
Epilogue **153**
    And Always the Waters 154
    Cold River Song 157
Appendix A: How Bad Was the Flood? 158
Appendix B: The Flood Chronology 160
Endnotes 163
Contributors 164

Preface

The Town of Alstead has experienced floods before along the Cold River and its tributary, Warren Brook, but the flood of October 9, 2005, was perhaps the greatest natural disaster to affect the town in its 242-year history. Virtually the entire population of the town was impacted by this event, in one way or another, through the loss of a home, loss of utilities, or isolation because of roads destroyed. Anyone who did not experience a direct economic loss knew a neighbor who did.

In the first days after the flood, members of the Alstead Historical Society (AHS) realized that the town had undergone a traumatic event that would have a lasting effect on the way residents viewed the Cold River and related to it. We believed that future generations would want to know what the flood was like, what it did to the town, and how our people responded. The flood needed to be documented.

Fall Mountain Regional High School students on field trip to the Alstead Historical Society. *Photograph by David Moody*

Fortuitously, the AHS had just received an invitation to apply for a Save Our History grant from television's History Channel. This program provides funds for historical societies to partner with local schools to inspire and motivate communities to learn about their past and to take an active role in preserving it. Several AHS members prepared the initial draft of an application for a grant. As soon as telephone service was restored, teachers were contacted at the Alstead Primary School, the Sarah Porter School (Langdon), the Vilas Middle School, the Fall Mountain Regional High School, and The Orchard School to discuss the proposal. By early November, we had a plan of action that involved teachers, students at all grade levels, and many members of the community in gathering information about the flood.

The overall objective of the project was to tell the story of the Alstead Flood of 2005 in words, oral histories, photographs, and art. The project proposal defined four major products:

Flood archives – Paper and electronic documents, news clippings, photographs, and oral histories that will serve as a resource for future research and study.

Museum exhibit – A display for the AHS Museum that shows photographs of homes before and after the flood on a map of the Warren Brook and the Cold River.

Fall Mountain Regional High School students briefed on collecting oral histories by Alstead Historical Society member Paul Rodrigue. *Photograph by David Moody*

Left to right: AHS members Lark Leonard, Erin Heidorn, Howard Weeks, and Carol Drummond work on the flood newsclippings archive folio. *Photograph by David Moody*

Photographic exhibit – A professionally mounted exhibition of selected photographs taken by residents during and after the flood that will be shown in various locations during 2006. Eventually it will be displayed in the AHS Museum.

Flood book – An illustrated commemorative volume that tells the story of the flood from the perspective of residents using their own words from the oral histories.

In mid-December, we received the welcome news that we would receive a *Save Our History* grant in the amount of $9,480. We received one of 26 grants awarded by the History Channel throughout the United States for 2005. We are grateful for this encouragement.

By January, a team of high school students had formed at the Fall Mountain Regional High School under the direction of teachers Taunya Lincoln (English) and William Ranauro (History). They immediately set out to collect oral histories using digital audio recorders purchased by AHS. These recordings were augmented by in depth interviews conducted by AHS members, Paul Rodrigue, and Lark Leonard during the spring. More than 100 interviews were done by the students, Lark, and Paul. High school students transcribed many of these.

At the same time, a call went out to the parents of all students in Alstead and surrounding towns for photographs of the flood and its aftermath. Tafi Brown, a local professional artist and independent curator for the photographic exhibition, started the difficult task of tracking down the photographers of the many images that we received. Interestingly, when people shared their CDs of digital pictures with us, they often contained a mix of personal pictures, pictures from

Artifacts collected from Millot Green archaeology project. *Photograph by David Germain*

High school students awaiting interviewees at the Shedd-Porter Memorial Library. *Photograph by David Moody*

relatives and friends, and images downloaded from the Internet. Tafi spent many hours sorting out who took which pictures. The result of her efforts and the generosity of people in and out of town who donated their pictures is an archive of more than 6,400 images. These will be displayed on a computer in the Shedd-Porter Memorial Library and as part of the AHS Museum exhibit.

A focal point of the Town of Alstead is the park – Millot Green. The Green has been the site of many historical activities. A paper mill flourished here along the Cold River in the late 18th and early 19th centuries drawn by the availability of waterpower. Civil War and World War I encampments took place on the Green in addition to numerous agricultural fairs over the years. Even today, Millot Green is the site of the annual Alstead Festival on the last weekend in July. The destruction of the recreational facilities on the Green provided an opportunity for metal detectionists and AHS members Greg Sherwood and David Germain to team up with 8th graders from Sharon Rabe's class at Vilas Middle School to engage in some industrial archaeology around the site of the paper mill. They discovered a large number of metal buttons, cut off and discarded from the worn garments used to make rag paper. They also found a variety of glass bottles, ceramic fragments, and clay pipe stems. We hope to continue this project with Vilas School in the coming year to further document the history of Millot Green.

AHS members Erin Heidorn, Cindy Hendrick, Carol Drummond, and Howard Weeks worked many evenings to organize scrapbooks of news clippings about the flood from local and regional newspapers. These clippings served as information resource for the authors and editors of this book.

In May 2006, our flood documentation project was selected as one of ten finalists to attend the Save Our History National Honors program in Washington, DC. Teachers Lincoln and Rabe accompanied four students — Cassandra Kreek, Ian Relihan, and Zackary Lincoln from Fall Mountain Regional High School and Zachary Whittaker from Vilas Middle School — on a memorable three-day trip to the Nation's capitol.

In June and July, the student editors, Cassandra Kreek, Ian Relihan, and Emily Kreek met with AHS members Lark Leonard, Jeanne Moody, David Moody, assisted from time to time by Tafi Brown, Cindy Hendrik, and Heather Gendron. Earlier in the year, high school student Nicole Varone also devoted considerable time to the project. While this is an AHS publication, it is very much the students' book. They organized the text, selected the flood

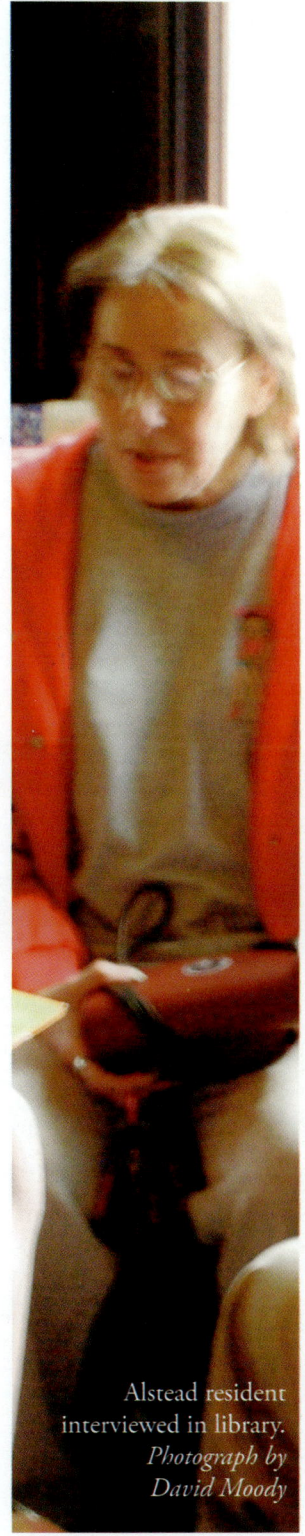

Alstead resident interviewed in library.
Photograph by David Moody

stories, and chose many of the photographs. Jeremy Townsend and Kat Mack of PublishingWorks provided considerably more than the usual amount of book design and editorial guidance—much of it on their own time. While it is impossible to recognize the work of all the students and friends who assisted in the project, we have attempted at the end of this book to acknowledge those who contributed. And of course the project could not have proceeded without the full support of the Alstead Historical Society's members and board of trustees.

The Town of Alstead will never be the same again after the flood of October 2005. As we think this book shows, we are a better and stronger town now despite the tragic loss of life, untold anguish over the destruction of homes, and the suffering of economic hardships. We are a hardy and resilient people. But, we learned that the generous spirit of neighbor helping neighbor extends well beyond the bounds of Alstead to other parts of New Hampshire, the nation, and the world. For this we are deeply grateful.

Is this the whole story of the Alstead flood? No. We have respected the need of many who experienced the flood to remain silent. The stories of their friends and neighbors, as documented in this book, represent only a few of the many experiences that have yet to be told. Our authors, documentary assistants, and students of all ages are to be commended for recording a complex and traumatic period in the history of the town. In the process they have learned much about the meaning of local history. We hope that some who read this volume will be inspired to share their own stories and images with us. We are always ready to listen. The story of the Alstead Flood – as with all history – will continue to unfold. We are grateful to be able to witness its narrative.

One more acknowledgement is worthy of note. Alexandra Lynn Kercewich, who was 5 years old at the time of the Alstead flood, provided the title of this book. When The Orchard School reopened the day after the flood, teacher Eleanor Elbers engaged her students in a group discussion of what had happened in Alstead the preceding weekend. In response to the question, "What is a flood?" Alex replied, in the succinct way of a true New Englander: "Too much water and too much rain!"

Bruce A. Bellows, **President**
Alstead Historical Society
July 31, 2006

The Waters

Overleaf:
The water above Alstead Village Bridge. Photograph by Mike Heidorn

A New Hampshire Hill Town

The Town of Alstead lies in the hills of northwest Cheshire County in Southwestern New Hampshire. The northern two-thirds of the town lies within the drainage of the Cold River, while the southern third lies in the Ashuelot River basin. Both streams are tributaries to the Connecticut River, the boundary between the states of New Hampshire and Vermont.

The founding of Alstead was successful only after false starts in 1735 and 1752. On the third attempt in 1763, the Provincial Governor of New Hampshire, Benning Wentworth, issued a charter to Samuel Chase and sixty-nine other proprietors and named the community Alstead. The boundaries of the town were promptly surveyed into lots of 250 acres plus an additional acre, called the "Town Lot." Each of the seventy proprietors was allocated a lot. The charter required that the town lots be located as closely as feasible to the geographic center of the town and were intended to cluster settlers for mutual protection against possible Indian raids. Eventually these town lots were laid out just to the northwest of Prentice Hill on a level piece of high ground now called Alstead Center.[1]

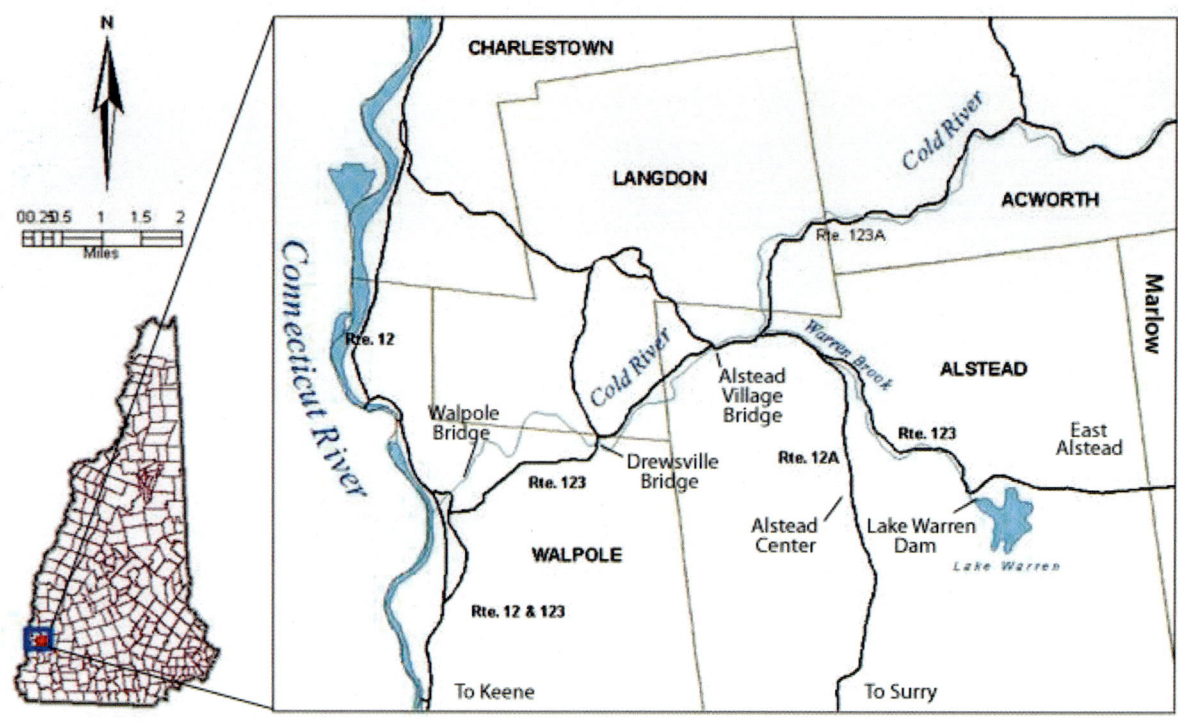

Location of Alstead, New Hampshire, and the Cold River. *Map courtesy of the New Hampshire Geological Survey*

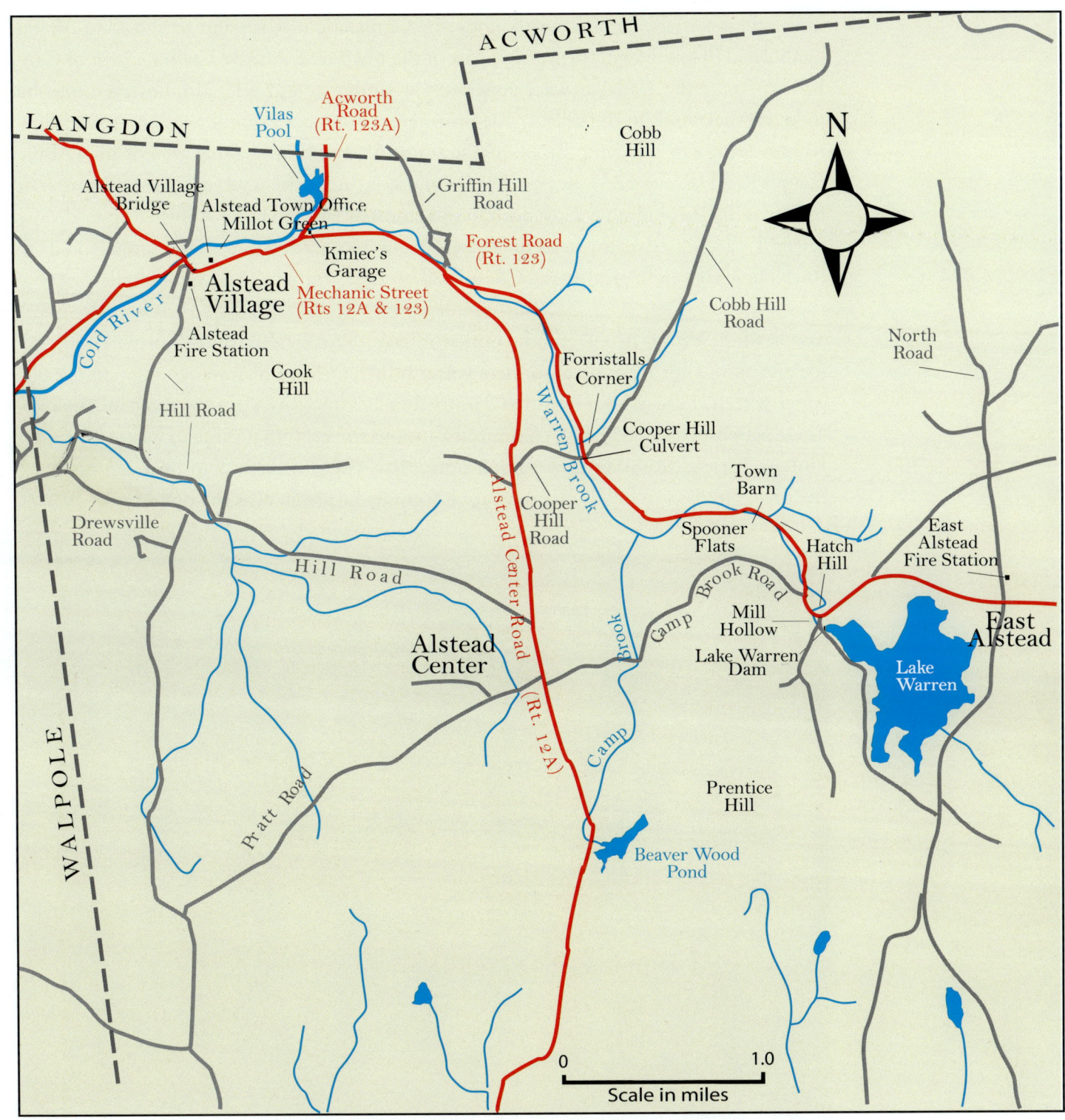

Location of roads, waterbodies, and place names in Alstead, New Hampshire, that are referred to in the text.

The earliest settlers, coming north along the Connecticut River and then east to Alstead, established themselves in the western part of the town or at Alstead Center, north of Camp Brook. To use the available water power to saw timber and grind grain, however, they had to locate their mills in the valleys. The proprietors located a sawmill with an up-and-down reciprocating saw on Camp Brook just south of Alstead Center along what is now Alstead Center Road (Route 12A). Beaver Wood Pond was one of the reservoirs used to store water for the mill. This mill may have been in operation as late as 1858.[2] Another up-and-down sawmill was located at the head of Warren Brook in East Alstead on the same land as the town's first grist mill.[3] Today, the Chase Mill occupies the site of that grist mill.

The head of Warren Brook and the outlet of Lake Warren (also called Warren Pond) were ideal locations for mills because there was a sufficient head of water to operate overshot water wheels. Lake Warren was first dammed in 1770 to provide a reservoir for the mills. These activities created a small community around the mills that came to be known as Mill Hollow. Alstead historian Helen Frink notes that "the clearest way to trace the history of the town's mills is to follow Warren Brook from its headwaters at the pond [Lake Warren]

Alstead Village ca. 1900 . *Photograph courtesy of Alstead Historical Society*

downstream past Forristalls Corner [the site of the Cooper Hill culvert] and into the Cold River."⁴ The steep gradient of Warren Brook and the regulated water supply from Lake Warren powered a succession of grist mills, carding and spinning mills, fulling mills, trip hammers, sawmills, and assorted wood shops manufacturing shingles, clothespins, and tool handles—all powered by water from the brook along Forest Road.

Farther downstream on the Cold River, Major Elisha Kingsbury built the first paper mill in New Hampshire in 1792 on the Cold River giving the name Paper Mill Village to the community that grew up around it. In 1793 he also built a brick sawmill on Mechanic Street [Newell's Mill], which is still standing. Over the next 100 years, the center of town affairs shifted from Alstead Center to Alstead Village (Paper Mill Village).

> The waterpower generated by Warren Brook and the Cold River determined a whole way of life in Alstead for a century and a half. A dozen millponds dotted the landscape.... Mill sites shaped the town's growth and development. Millhands needed lodging and often rented temporary

The Brick Mill, built in 1793 by Kingsbury, known as Newell's Mill on Mechanic Street ca. 1900.
Photograph courtesy of Alstead Historical Society

quarters. The boarding house they occupied would later fill with summer boarders as the mill workers' numbers declined...Today most of Alstead's mills have vanished, but the cluster of houses in a hollow beside a stream and roadway remain to remind us of their importance.

In 1828, Forest Road, an early route that connected Bellows Falls, Vermont, and Marlow, New Hampshire, was relocated from what is now the western part of Camp Brook Road, to its present location along the length of Warren Brook. This provided a more direct route between East Alstead and Paper Mill Village and also took advantage of better grades and road alignments. Forest Road was graveled in the 1920s and black-topped in the 1930s. It is now N.H. State Route 123. In 1870 Paper Mill Village officially changed its name to Alstead.

At the end of the 19th century, city dwellers were attracted by the pastoral ambience of Alstead, the waters of Lake Warren, and the fields of Alstead Center. With the growth of automobile use, these areas became the centers of summer colonies. Many of these summer residents eventually moved to Alstead year-round.

Shedd-Porter Memorial Library (left) and Maybelle H. Still building (right). *Photograph by David Moody.*

Population fell, as with most small New England towns, during the 19th century from a high of 1,694 residents in 1810 to about 800 in 1900 and 616 in 1930. Only in 1990 did Alstead's population exceed its peak population and reach 1,721.[6] At present (2006) Alstead has slightly under 2,000 residents.

What is Alstead then? A rural New England village with fewer than two thousand villagers? A picturesque retreat? An old mill town that had seen better days? A cheerful place, a quiet place, home.

It really depends on whom you ask. For Dale Dustin, the nature of Alstead is rooted in the past. The Alstead of his youth in the 1940's was "a quaint village" inspiring vivid memories of haying with horses, brownie sundaes, a local barber, and old-style telephones. Tammy Gendron, too, has fond memories of her childhood in the town:

> It was just - how do I describe it? It was just people! It was a great place to grow up. I guess it was a place where everybody knew everybody. I used to pasture my pony on neighbors' lawns. I grew up behind the library here in town. We roller-skated in the road, rode our bikes. I was 7 years old with my best friend, Amanda, roller-skating, and Erwin Ward [the police chief] told us we had to stop...We were breaking up the road!

Memorial Day procession to war memorial at Millot Green, May 2003. *Photograph by David Moody.*

James Fowle, who has lived along the Cold River since he was a boy, could tell you the history of his town. He now lives in a house that used to be a tavern, a market, and a boarding house. Its landlord owned the Newell Mill about two hundred feet upstream which was once a sawmill then a grist mill. Millot Green, the town's common, offers linguistic evidence: "It was Mill Lot Green," explains Jim, "because it was all mill lots, so over the years it got shortened to Millot Green." But soon the large towns became regional centers of commerce and manufacturing. Bellow Falls, Vermont, gained control of the paper industry while Keene, New Hampshire, and Springfield, Vermont, took over the machine shops. The pace of the town that once boasted a blacksmith and a paper mill, a coach shop and a hotel slowed down. Alstead shifted quietly into a more modest role with a large assortment of farms, greenhouses, and cottage industries.

Some modern-day local businesses have flourished—Tammy's Brick Shop Floral, Joe's Citgo, Benson Woodworking, Blanchflower Lumber, Fuller Machine Company, and Tory Hill Glass & Restoration—to name a few. The Alstead Village Market, the town's general store, provides a hub for the subdued bustle of small-town life.

Alstead Festival on Millot Green, July 2005. *Photograph by Cindy Hendrick*

Across the street is Millot Green. Remnants of its industrial heritage are buried beneath green turf, soccer nets, a basketball court, and a horse ring that had just been refurbished the spring of 2005. This is the location of the annual Alstead Festival, a "celebration of who we are and a time to see people," says Lark Leonard. Come July, families from all corners of Alstead gather to enjoy live music, games, crafts, and other festivities. Community events like this often unite Alstead's residents. The Orchard School in East Alstead has become another popular gathering place for area children and families. Alstead is also the center of the district-wide Friendly Meals which, under the loving guidance of Mary Lou Huffling, serves hundreds of meals to senior citizens each week.

Dairy farming, maple syrup production, and vegetable farming now play a relatively minor role in the town's economy. Many residents commute to jobs in nearby communities, such as Keene. Yet all highly value the rural character of the small hill town.

Mary Lou Huffling prepares a community meal. *Photograph by Ole Bye, courtesy of* The Eagle Times, *October 24, 2005.*

Cold River

The Cold River connects eight small, rural towns in New Hampshire (Unity, Charlestown, Lempster, Acworth, Alstead, Langdon, and Walpole) as it flows from its source in Crescent Lake in Unity, 23.5 mi to its mouth on the Connecticut River in Walpole. It has a drainage area of 102 square miles (sq mi). During its journey, the river drops 985 feet (ft) through deep valleys. A digital elevation model of the basin shows the rough texture of the landscape.

In 1999, the New Hampshire General Court (legislature) recognized the Cold River as a significant natural, cultural, scenic, and scientific resource by making the Cold River a Designated River, one of only fourteen such rivers in the state. Upon designation, the Cold River became part of the New Hampshire Rivers Management and Protection Program (RMPP), a partnership between the state and local communities and citizens. A local river corridor management plan is being developed for the basin by the Cold River Local Advisory Committee, which is made up of volunteer representatives from five of the basin's towns.[7]

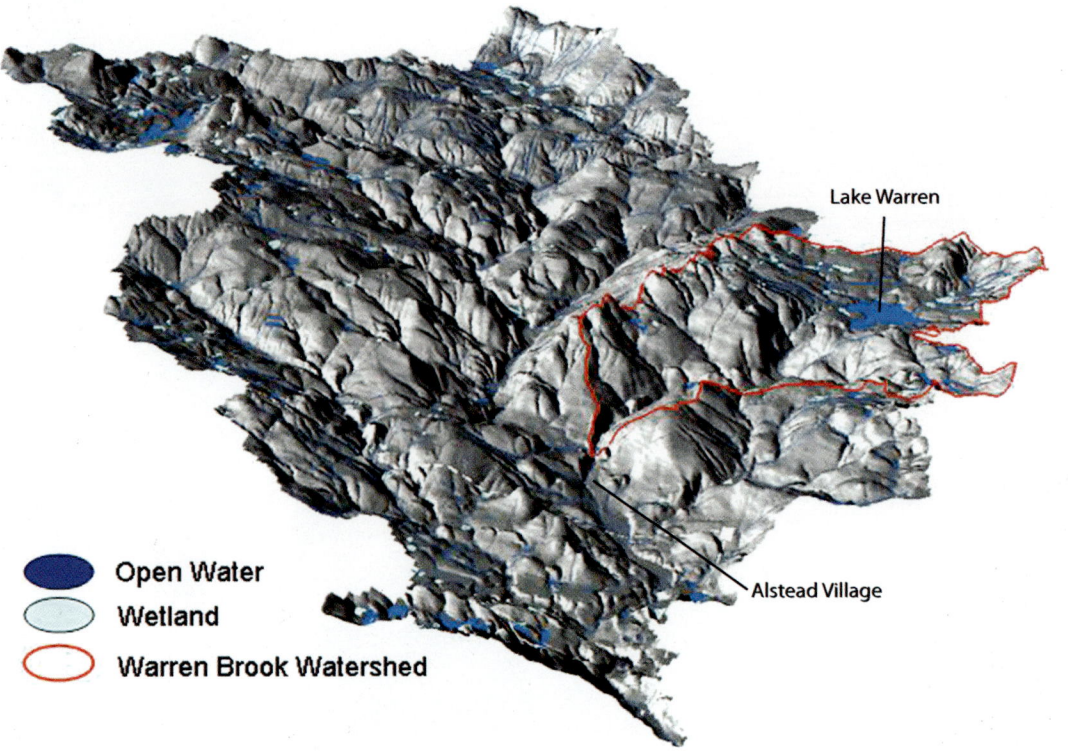

Topography (digital elevation model) of the Cold River basin. *Courtesy of the New Hampshire Geological Survey*

As part of its efforts, the Cold River Local Advisory Committee undertook a water quality characterization project in 2002. Since then, physical, chemical, and biological measurements are made periodically at twenty-eight key sites in the basin. The water quality is generally good to excellent with a few areas characterized as poor. The river is widely known as an excellent cold-water trout stream and is used by canoeists and kayakers for recreational purposes. Many people in Alstead remember a favorite swimming hole.

Two large sub-watersheds (Grassy Brook and Dart Brook), which drain the eastern and southern parts of Alstead to the Ashuelot River, contain wetlands, riparian zones, and large undivided forest ecosystems that The Nature Conservancy has identified as a major opportunity to conserve large unfragmented ecosystems.[8] Many other areas in the Cold River basin contain similar natural features.

Flowing along Route 123A, the Cold River passes through Acworth and enters Alstead. Just over the town line, the Vilas Pool Dam impounds the river to form Vilas Pool (6 acres in area). The pool, a gift of Alstead benefactor Charles Nathaniel Vilas in 1926, serves Alstead as a recreation area and park. Usually water flows through a gate in the lower part of the dam or over the dam's spillway. Occasionally during floods, water will flow out of the pool and down Acworth Road, bypassing the dam.

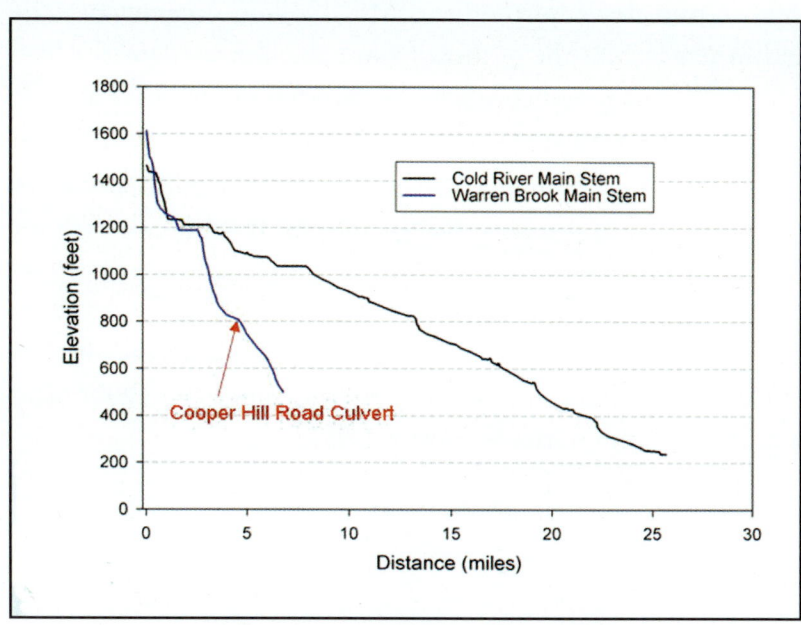

Comparison of the slopes of the Cold River and the much steeper Warren Brook. *Courtesy of the New Hampshire Geological Survey*

The river continues through a small gorge below the pool and there is joined by the Warren Brook, 6.45 mi upstream of the Connecticut River. From its confluence with the Warren Brook, the Cold River flows in an easterly direction paralleling Mechanic Street, passes a rock formation in the stream channel called "The Ledges" and then along the Newell (Kingsbury) Mill and Millot Green. Here the river flows under the Alstead Village Bridge, 5.81 mi from the Connecticut. A straight reach of river channel extends for a half mile below Alstead Village along River Street (called Cold River Road in Langdon) and then meanders past several large agricultural fields until it reaches the Drewsville Bridge (Rt. 123) at 3.50 mi upstream of its mouth. Here the U.S. Geological Survey operated a stream-gaging station 60 ft upstream of the bridge between 1940 and 1978. The drainage area of the basin at this point is 82.7 sq mi. Then the Cold River plunges 25 ft into Drewsville Gorge and finally passes the site of the North Walpole Bridge 0.33 mi above its mouth and finally passes under the Route 12 bridge. It discharges into the Connecticut River at an elevation of 230 ft. The average slope of the Cold River between Vilas Pool and its mouth is fairly steep, averaging about 45 ft/mi.[9]

Warren Brook

The main stem of Warren Brook has its headwaters on the east flank of Prentice Hill, at elevations of about 1,500 ft. and flows northerly to Mill Hollow, a center of early industrial activity in Alstead, where it joins the outflow from Lake Warren dam, a 170-ft long, 10-ft high structure of stone, earth, and concrete. A dam has existed here as early as 1772 to provide a reservoir for water-powered mills on Warren Brook. The dam was recently reconstructed in 1993 with a 2.5 ft high x 29 ft wide spillway.[10] The watershed draining into Lake Warren drains 4.87 sq mi. It is exactly 4.50 mi from the dam to the mouth of Warren Brook.

Lake Warren (Warren Pond) is the largest water body in Alstead with an area of 186 acres and has been the location of a thriving summer community since the 1900s. This corner of East Alstead has many fond memories for Alstead residents.

I associate Warren Brook with the first tree swallows of spring (they always gather by the dam) and with wading; with Heman Chase throwing open the sluice at the Mill and teaching woodworking to children, the Mill door left wide open, using waterpower to run the saws. I have heard the ice of many springtimes break over the dam, the crash and roar of the water now freed to flow, and I have watched the mosaic of autumn leaves in the dark water--carrying their brightness downstream.

Once, when I was lucky, I witnessed the moment of the dragonfly hatching all around the cove by Warren Dam. The air, which had been empty, was suddenly filled with lifting wings. I felt I had been included in a very private moment. So you see, the waters have always been a lovely part of my life--lyrical, always interesting, to be respected but never to be feared.

Lark Leonard

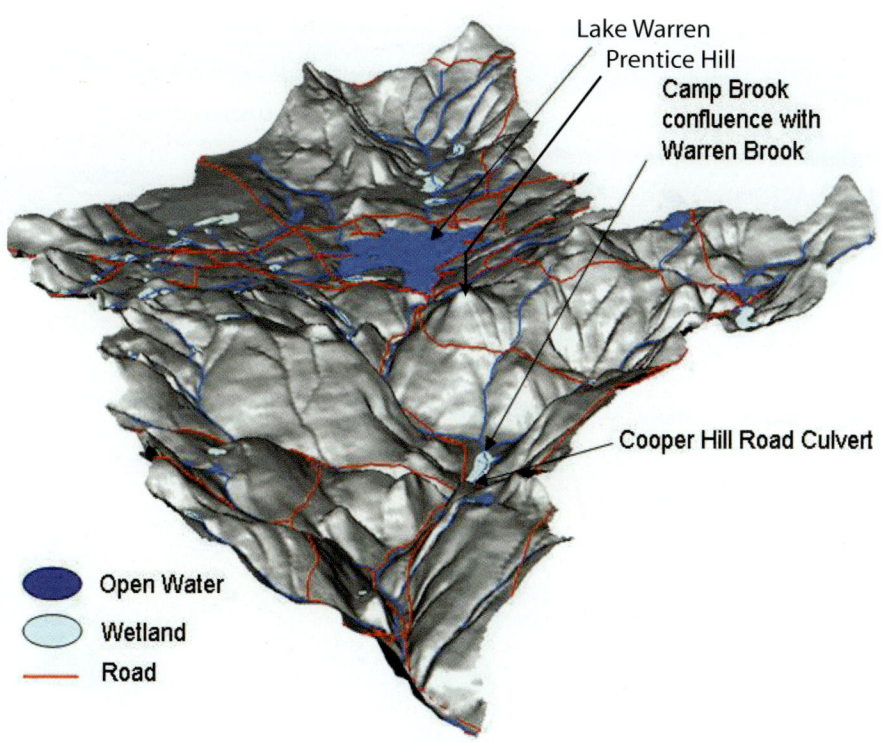

Topography (digital elevation model) of the Warren Brook basin.
Courtesy of the New Hampshire Geological Survey

THE CULVERT

John Burroughs remembers a green iron bridge that spanned Warren Brook at Forristalls Corner prior to 1968.[11] The bridge had stone abutments and stood about 22 feet above the bed of the brook. Erosion of the bridge's abutments caused the bridge to fail in 1966. In the 1967 *Town Report*, the Selectmen stated: "The bridge on Cooper Hill has let us down and we must do something about it. We are thinking about a culvert instead of another bridge…."[12]

A 6-foot diameter, bolted, metal culvert was purchased from the R.C. Hazelton Company in 1968 and installed with great difficulty.[13] Evidently, the culvert was too short for the site, and heavy rains caused the slopes of the embankment above the culvert to slide and obstruct it. John Burroughs recalls that the culvert's header became obstructed during the spring flood of 1969 and collapsed. Water backed up and overtopped the low point in the tar road. According to his diary, on June 18, 1969, John Burroughs and Frank Jenks dug out the old culvert with a bulldozer and "lowered the brook." The Hazelton Company offered to replace the culvert.[14]

The town warrant for 1970 asked the town to approve applying for State Bridge aid to build a new "bridge" (culvert) at Cooper Hill. A 12-foot diameter metal culvert, 110-feet long on its bottom side, was installed in the summer of 1971. The road surface was approximately 30 feet above the bed of Warren Brook. The selectmen reported that "the bridge at the foot of Cooper Hill was completed under the supervision of the State Highway [sic]. It is noted that this road is receiving much usage…"[15]

In 1989, Road Agent Ken Winham reported that the Cooper Hill culvert was eroding on the outlet side during the weekend of October 20. He recommended that the bank be repaired by placing riprap stone. In his report of 1991, he said: "Cooper Hill was riprapped and the bank replaced at a cost of $3,200. I hope it holds this time."[16]

Passing through the millpond and dam of Chase's Mill, Warren Brook literally plunges down Hatch Hill at a slope of about 332 ft/mi to the bridge near its foot. Most of the early water-powered mills, such as the Hatch (Kidder) sawmill, were located along this reach of the brook. In contrast, Warren Brook has an average slope of 57 ft/mi along Spooner Flats to Cooper Hill Road. At the downstream end of Spooner Flats, the brook passes under Cooper Hill Road through a 12-ft diameter, 110 ft long metal culvert. From just below the confluence with Allen Brook (Mad Brook), Warren Brook again descends steeply to the Cold River at a slope of 227 ft/mi.

> Warren Brook begins as the outlet to Lake Warren, flowing over the dam, through Mill Hollow, down through a little gorge where several mills once operated and onward northwest about four miles where it joins Cold River in Alstead...
>
> In spring the brook is full and rushes along. In summer there is much less water. The motion is slower; the water gurgles past grasses, mossy stone, and fallen trees...In late summer, the water is likely to be at its lowest. There may be only a little trickle in Warren Brook and some of its little tributaries dry up completely.
>
> *Margaret Chase Perry*

Camp Brook rises on the western slope of Prentice Hill, passes westward through Beaver Wood Pond and under Alstead Center Road (Route 12A) into a large beaver meadow. From there, it flows east again back under Alstead Center Road past the site of the early Camp Brook sawmill and through a steep valley to another beaver pond on the south side of Camp Brook Road (Log Cabin Road). Here the brook passes under Camp Brook Road through a pair of barrel culverts, down a steep valley to join Warren Brook on the south side of Spooner Flats just above Cooper Hill Road.

> I used to hear thousands of frogs calling back and forth from the valley to the south of the Cooper Hill culvert. I heard wonderful choruses of spring peepers; wood frogs that sound like ducks; American toads with their long, musical trill; green frogs that call like Kermit's 'gunk'; and grey tree frogs that throw their short trill so it sounds like they are sitting right next to you.
>
> *Carol Drummond*

The recent geologic history of the Cold River is a fascinating story in itself. Some 12,000 years ago, the retreating ice sheet that covered much of New England dammed the ancestral Connecticut River to form Lake Hitchcock. Glacial meltwater, discharging into the lake, deposited many of the thick layers of sand and gravel that are mined today in the Drewsville area for aggregate. The ancestral Cold River eroded downward through glacial sand and gravel deposits and till and eroded into the bedrock in locations such as Vilas Pool, Alstead Village, and Drewsville Gorge. The meandering river also eroded a series of terraces found on both sides of the river as it cut deeper into the valley. Cross sections of the terraces that resulted from this downcutting can be seen today on the high bank along Warren Brook on the north side of Forest Road below its intersection with Alstead Center Road (Rt. 12A) and on the bank on the north side of the Cold River along Mechanic Street.[17]

As a stream flows downhill it dissipates its energy by eroding the boundaries of its channel and transporting sediment. Over time, natural streams reach a dynamic equilibrium between the water discharge and the sediment discharge. The equilibrium condition indicates that the stream alignment, channel geometry (width, depth, and slope), and sediment load are in balance. Parts of the channel in a particular reach of stream may be eroding at the same time that sediments are being deposited in other parts of the channel. Generally, the shape of the channel will be stable, but the location of the channel may not be. In the downstream direction, natural channels characteristically have riffles (rapidly

Backyard of the Wilson property along Warren Brook before the flood.
Photograph by Bobbie Wilson.

flowing, shallow stream segments) alternating with more slowly flowing pools. These pools and riffles, well known to fishermen, are important to the aquatic habitat of a stream. During floods, the streambed and banks may undergo severe erosion that alters the channel width, depth, and slope. It may take many months or years for equilibrium to be reestablished in a channel. The stream may attempt to meander to lengthen the stream reach and thereby decrease the stream slope. In the process of meandering, streambanks erode. Attempts to stabilize part of a streambank and make it immovable by using riprap or ledge rock deprives the stream of sediment in that reach and will likely transfer the area of erosion to another location. Similarly, attempts to modify the shape of the channel may have far-reaching effects both upstream and downstream of the modified channel. Analysis of the fluvial geometry of the stream is needed to understand the local stream dynamics and to prevent costly errors in river restoration efforts.

The Cold River historically has been known as a flashy stream. The generally thin soils underlain by impermeable bedrock or compact glacial till on steep hill slopes when combined with heavy, intense rainfall can quickly lead to sudden-flood conditions. Major regional floods occurred in the basin in April 1852; November 1927; March 1936 (rain and snow melt); September 1938 (hurricane); July and December 1973, July to August 1986, September 1999 (Hurricane Floyd), and most recently, October 2005.

The severity of floods is often expressed by their peak flow, the maximum instantaneous discharge of a stream at a particular location. By analyzing the historic annual peak floods, hydrologists can develop a statistical expression of how often a flood or rainfall of a given magnitude will, on the average, be equaled or exceeded. Thus, we hear about the 50-year flood, or the 100-year 24-hour rainfall. The depth of flooding by a 100-year flood can be shown on a topographic map. The area inundated by the 100-year flood is called the 100-year floodplain. Unfortunately, this measure of severity is often misunderstood by the general public. The erroneous perception is that once a 100-year flood has occurred, there will not be another flood of that size for another hundred years. The measure actually represents a statistical average. While improbable, it is quite possible to have several 100-year flood events in a row.

People like to live on the banks of rivers for a variety of reasons. However, in doing so they take a risk of being flooded. It is important to know where you live in relation to a river's floodplain and to understand the risk that you assume by living there.

Storm Brewing

A tropical disturbance formed east of the Bahamas on October 3, 2005, and moved landward toward Florida. On October 5, the storm was named "Tammy," the nineteenth named storm of the Atlantic hurricane season. Tammy moved north over Georgia on October 6 and then veered south and dissipated over the Florida Panhandle, an unremarkable storm as far as tropical storms go.

Tammy's importance to Alstead, far to the north, was its influence in transporting enormous amounts of tropical moisture northward. A slowly moving cold front from the Midwest lifted the tropical moist air in a narrow zone along the eastern seaboard. The resulting heavy rainfall of October 6-9 stretched a thousand miles from the Carolinas to New England. Precipitation amounts ranged from 3 to 7 inches with isolated amounts in excess of 12 inches.[18] Alstead's October 2005 flood was born.

Tropical Storm Tammy over the eastern United States on October 7, 2005. The west coast of Florida can be seen in the bottom center of the image. Nova Scotia is located at the top right. *GOES-12 satellite image courtesy of the National Oceanic and Atmospheric Administration (NOAA)*

The good news is that the flooding could have been worse. In the first week of October, New England was beginning to suffer from drought conditions. Soils were unusually dry, streams were experiencing low flows, and well levels were falling. During October 7-9, the remnants of Tropical Storm Tammy moved along the cold front, now stalled over New England, and traveled up the Connecticut River valley. Moist air was forced upwards onto the hills surrounding the valley and enhanced precipitation over hill towns such as Alstead. The heaviest precipitation occurred on the tributaries of the Connecticut River between North Walpole, New Hampshire, and Greenfield, Massachusetts.[19] Had not the soil been dry, the amount of runoff resulting from the storm could have been considerably greater. Subsequent storms of October 14-15 and October 25 set records for the precipitation in October in many parts of southern New England.

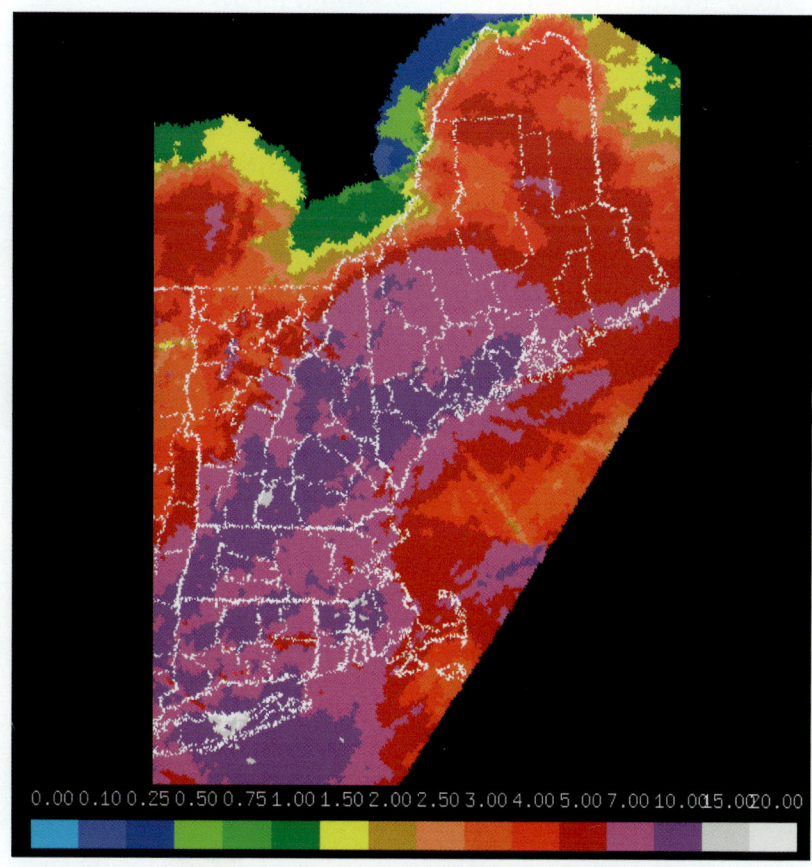

Estimated cumulative rainfall for the period October 7-16, 2005 obtained by National Weather Service radars (NEXRAD). Dark purple areas indicated rainfall in excess of 10 inches; gray indicated rainfall in excess of 15 inches. *Image courtesy of the National Weather Service, National Oceanic and Atmospheric Administration*

It began raining at the Klein place in East Alstead at 7:00 p.m. on Friday, October 7. Gaale Klein is a volunteer weather observer whose reports are often heard on the "Eye in the Sky" weather reports several times a day on Vermont Public Radio. By midnight on October 8, East Alstead had received a total of 7.50 inches of rain, well exceeding the estimated 100-year 24-hour rainfall of 6.10 inches. On the west side of Prentice Hill at Beaver Wood Pond as much as 8 inches may have fallen.[20]

By Sunday morning, October 9, at 7:00 a.m. locations in or near Alstead recorded the following cumulative amounts of rain during the preceding 36 hours:[21]

East Alstead (G. Klein)	10.24 inches
Alstead Center (S. Sutcliffe)	>10.50 inches
Beaver Wood Pond (D. Moody)	10.80 inches
Walpole (NCDC)	9.84 inches

Most of the Cold River Watershed received at least 10 to 10.5 inches of rain during the weekend of October 7-9, 2005, nearly one quarter of the average annual rainfall of 42 inches for the basin.[22] Cumulative rainfall for the period October 7-16 totaled 14.56 inches for East Alstead. A colorful display prepared by the National Weather Service Office in Gray, Maine, based on NWS radar data, shows the cumulative amounts of rainfall in New England for the 240-hour period from October 7 to October 17. The gray rectangular area over the northwest part of Cheshire County, represents an accumulation of between 15 and 20 inches of precipitation. This gray area covers much of the town of Alstead and the Cold River basin.

Floodwatch

"It was peaceful the night before the flood. I was asleep, and all I heard was the sound of rain on a tin roof."

~Grace Rushing (age 11)

Overleaf: Stella Winham's home on Forest Road. *Photograph by Margaret Gacek*

Friday

October 7, 2005, was like most October days. The foliage was nearing peak color, the children were in school, and most people were out and about their usual Friday activities. It was early in the evening when the rain moved in. Even so, it had been an unusually wet autumn, and no one thought much of it.

Storm clouds over Mechanic Street, Alstead. *Photograph by Kathy Torrey*

Saturday

It hadn't stopped raining, but most of Alstead seemed to be out-of-town or out-on-the-town that Saturday evening. It was the night of Benson's Clambake, and Selectman Joel McCarty was enjoying himself—"drinking beer, listening to a pretty good band." The town's two other selectmen were out of state: Bill Moran was in a hospital in New York, and Matt Saxton was taking the day off.

> It was great fun, because I was in Boston at a matinee play in the afternoon and a fabulous dinner out somewhere in South Boston. It was raining just a little bit but not enough to ruin our good time with such great friends. We were having a grand outing.

In East Alstead, Orchard School teacher Eleanor Elbers was hosting guests. "We actually had this huge event… A world-renowned author just happened to be staying at our farm." Eleanor was also babysitting for a couple from Seattle. They were heading to a concert in Brattleboro with Eleanor's husband, Anton, and for the first time ever, were leaving their son in someone else's care.

Police chief Christopher Lyons was planning to begin a nine-day vacation at midnight—his first vacation in two years. "So I could do that, I was typing up my paperwork in the office. It was a good night to do it because it was raining and there wasn't a lot of traffic out." Fire Chief Kim Kercewich meanwhile was in Franklin, New Hampshire, at a forest-fire training workshop. Kim's son, Mike Kercewich, and his wife Jodi, were relaxing in a Chinese restaurant after a day of work. Another couple—Matt and Julie Goodell—spent the rainy Saturday in a shopping mall. Still others, like Friendly Meal coordinator Mary Lou Huffling, were heading to the Third Congregational Church for their Harvest Auction.

The only one who seemed to be paying much attention to the rain was David Crosby, and that was not unusual: it was part of his job. Previously the town's Road Agent, now called the Public Works Director, David started work at three o'clock that afternoon, checking trouble spots in the town's roads and culverts. Because there is never enough money to go around and repair everything at once, there are always areas that need to be watched. This was almost routine: he was worried, but not too worried.

Except the rain didn't stop. It saturated the ground and collected in puddles, gushing into the dozens of little brooks that wound their way down into the valley. Klaus Bayr, professor of geography at Keene State College, knew that so much rain posed a threat: "The land was soaked, the soil was soaked, so where should all the water go?"

5:00 P.M.

Matt Goodell came home from the mall late that afternoon. "I noticed that the river was extremely high, higher than I can ever remember seeing it. And I've grown up in this area for years and years." The Goodell family had recently moved to 91 River Street. "I'd always joked to my wife that we'd never have to worry about a flood, because it's like a little dam there, so we're protected." But when they walked over to the river, the water was level with the top of the embankment. "I didn't say anything to my wife at the time. I was thinking to myself, *Oh, this is not good*."

> In October there was a flood stirring up.
>
> ~Michaela Gabardi (age 12)

Anton Elbers drove off at about six o'clock, leading his Seattle friends' car over the Flats at the foot of Hatch Hill. He was surprised to find them already flooding, and he thought, there must be water really backing up somewhere. As always, he carried his pager. As an EMT working for the Alstead ambulance, he had to be on the alert. He made it to the concert without any problems although something unusual happened: "The power went out in the middle of the concert for half an hour…these guys brought flashlights onto the stage, and they just kept right on playing, and it was wonderful."

Mike and Jodi were on their way back from the Chinese restaurant. "Let's go back through the Camp Brook way, " suggested Mike, who is on the highway crew. When the couple found six to eight inches of water on the road, Mike knew something was up:

> I looked at [Jodi] and I said, "This ain't good; this is not good. If this rain don't let up, this road's going to be gone. Whatever else behind it, who knows." As I headed up…I met the state guy who's out of Marlow, and I stopped and rolled down the window and joking around a little (he's putting out HIGH WATER signs)…I says, "Ah, you're finally out doin' somethin'?"
>
> He says, "You know, this isn't good. I've got this gut feeling that something's going to go wrong tonight. I don't know what…just be aware…

Left to right: Fire Chief Kim Kercewich, Road Agent David Crosby, Police Chief Christopher Lyons in front of Lake Warren Dam. *Photograph by Michael Moore, courtesy of* The Keene Sentinel, *October 27, 2005.*

Chief Lyons was still at work in the police station in the basement of the Alstead Municipal Offices building at the edge of Millot Green when he received a phone call from someone who had almost gone off the road at Forristalls Corners—the intersections of Forest Road, Cobb Hill, and Cooper Hill Road. This was often the first place to flood, and Chris decided to check out the situation to be safe. At 7:07 another call reported flooding at the dam on Pine Cliff Road, making it all but impassible. This was now town responsibility. Concerned about the little wooden bridge at Prentice Hill, Chris decided it was time to contact David Crosby.

David was uneasy. It was then—a little after seven o'clock—that he began to suspect the severity of the events that were about to unfold. Not only was the state road flooding, as Chief Lyons had just witnessed, but the small culvert right above the Town Barn [garage] where Warren Brook runs under Route 123 had clogged with sticks, trees, and other debris. By eight o'clock, David would be forced to close off Hatch Hill entirely and make a detour over Camp Brook Road. Now, David and Chris decided it would be best to evacuate the area across from the Town Barn.

Town barn (highway garage) on Forest Road. *Photograph by Jeanne Moody*

Meanwhile, Eleanor Elbers was still home in East Alstead with her friends' baby.

> Then I heard a knock on the door. It was a close friend who was trying to get home from up on North Road from Gilsum. And she said, "I can't go anywhere! I tried to go up to Marlow and there was just like a hundred feet of water! I don't think I can go through it; I don't know how deep it is…I feel like I'm stuck. I definitely can't go this way because the road is closed." I was puzzled.

> It's hard to think about what happened so I call it *remembering the unbelievable*.
>
> ~Sara DeValk (age 11)

"The road is closed?"

"The road down to the village is closed!" she said.

"Route 123 is closed?" I asked. By this time it was 8:30.

"Yeah, there's a sign that says HIGH WATER!"

Eleanor was not the only one who was surprised to hear of the night's happenings. Earlier in the evening, Chief Lyons had stopped in to see his friend John Anderson who jokingly persuaded him that things would be fine: "Come on! Nothing ever happens in Alstead… We can go out to Bellows Falls and get a Dunkin' Donut and ride around; I've always wanted to ride in a real cruiser and get a donut with a real cop." But when Chris explained the situation, John asked on a more serious note, "Do you want some company tonight?"

After the Andersons' dinner, Chris returned to pick up his friend, and together they headed down Hatch Hill to begin the evacuations. "I worked [Route] 123 back and forth for hours…I lost track," remembers Chris, "The night—it was like you were on a fast Six Flags ride, and it just keeps right on going; it doesn't stop."

9:00 P.M.

Almut Yakovleff decided to go to bed in her home on Mechanic Street. "There were a couple of times in my at-least twenty years of living here that the river had been high, and I used to have sleepless nights and worry and pace and wonder what to pack and what to do. And so I've taught myself that just because the river's high you can relax, and it will be all right."

In East Alstead, Eleanor Elbers had put her friends' child to bed when there was another knock at her door:

> Another friend was trying to get home… She made it up over Marlow Hill, but she couldn't get to the village…it was about nine o'clock, and I was like whoa crazy; I called Anton again and I said,
> "The road—"
> "I've just been told. I'm coming into the village. I'll call you when I get there."
> [Anton] arrives at the fire station, and this young couple whose child is with me (asleep) says, "We have to get home to our baby!" … I am wondering, *how bad can this be?*

It had been raining harder when Anton left Brattleboro, Vermont, at about 9:30 P.M. and headed home. He could not cross the Connecticut River over the bridge at Westminster, so he was continuing north through Bellows Falls when his monitor toned to announce that Hatch Hill would be closing. Then, just as he drove by Kmiec's Garage, it toned a second time to call all ambulance and fire personnel to the East Alstead and Alstead Village fire stations. Unable to accompany his friends home, he told Eleanor he would send the couple around through Keene, down Route 12 and up Route 10. Eleanor was skeptical, and replied, "Okay, good luck. Well, good luck to them. I mean they don't know the area at all!"

They were not the only ones who would be driving around that night. "There were people getting stranded right and left," Anton remembers. High school senior Grace Perry and her boyfriend Pat were heading home from a party at the Gendrons' house when they hit high waters. "The rest of road was covered in about two inches of water, so we couldn't tell until we were in it, that it was like two feet deep, and it just washed right over the car." Afraid to face the water behind them—for safety's sake and for the sake of Pat's new car—the two pressed on and eventually made it to Grace's home on Bennett Road.

Courtney Porter was not so lucky. She was coming home to her house on Main Street from Laconia when she got stranded. "I was actually pulled over, freaking out, because I had never driven through moving water before, and I didn't have my own car. I had a friend's very little car, and [the water] came right up over the hood. So I got a phone call from people with a big truck, bigger than my car, saying, 'Stay where you are! We'll come get you.' And they never came, and they never came, and they never came!"

East Alstead Fire Station. *Photograph by Jeanne Moody*

> *"What I thought was thunder really was the river moving huge rocks."*
>
> *~Lyle Doolittle (age 12)*

> *When the culvert broke, there were huge waves that caused rocks, trees, and houses to break into pieces.*
>
> *~Jarid Crosby (age 12)*

Matt Goodell was also driving through water after his sump-pump had begun overflowing. "I was concerned because it was within probably two inches of the top of the hole, and being that we had just built the house, the majority of everything we owned was downstairs in the basement." It was about 10:30 p.m. when Matt left to pick up another pump from a friend. He came to the bridge just past Route 12A where Forest Road intersects Warren Brook. Water was already coming over its edges. It was one of those things where I was in kind of a panic situation to get this pump. So you're driving through water that you are always told not to drive through, but I made it. And he made it through three or four more questionable spots and picked up his pump. "I got home and stuff was floating everywhere. My wife was crying." Needless to say, Matt would be back on the road again that night, searching frantically for more pumps.

David Crosby, meanwhile, was dealing with water on a larger scale. "As the night went on, things kept getting worse and worse and worse." At about ten o'clock, he noticed that the Spooner Flats below the Town Barn were filling with water.

> That happens too. I've seen that a dozen times in the twenty-three or twenty-four years I've worked here. That's not an uncommon thing. But it usually stops raining, and this time it didn't.

While others were focusing on the evacuations, he continued to keep an eye on the road, especially on the culverts, pulling out branches and other debris to keep the water flowing. It was a challenge to simply see in the dark. "You have to use flashlights and the headlights on your truck. You position your trucks so you can do what you have to do." Yet more and and more roads were becoming impassable.

Matt Saxton was heading home. He had returned from Boston to his friend's house in Gilsum to pick up his car.

> At about 10:30 Saturday night I said my goodbyes, got in my car, and I got all the way to Chase's Mill where I met a fire truck and Don Martin and Jodi Kercewich who told me that I probably couldn't get further. I said, "Well, come on."
> And they said, "Well look."
> And they shone their light down toward the Tinker barn, and there was water, oh, a foot deep, rushing diagonally in the general direction of Tom Hancock's house. In my Boston go-to-the-city shoes and my socks and

slacks, Don and I waded out into that to see that the water was actually under the pavement; it had bubbled the pavement up. We decided that I certainly couldn't drive through that, and we were sure that I wouldn't get around the back way either, so I went back to Gilsum to spend the night there…I called Chief Lyons and I said,

"You know, the nightmare disaster scenario is if the bottom of Cooper Hill lets go."

11:00 P.M.

Matt Saxon was not the only one who was concerned. Chief Lyons was actually standing at the base of Cooper Hill as he was talking to Matt. "I know, I know," he said, "we are monitoring this." The culvert was actually not clogged with debris—and would never be clogged that night—as Kim Kercewich was eager to explain. "It is a twelve-foot squash pipe (that means it is oval) and the water is about five feet above the top of that. The road is probably twenty-five to thirty feet above the pipe. So I went over to the outlet end, and there was only about three feet of room above the water, which is about as much as the pipe can take." The force of the water building up behind the culvert posed a threat to the

Water rushing down Hatch Hill towards Thomas Hancock's place. *Photograph by Margaret Perry*

> It was real scary when we had to leave the night of the flood, but I was glad we left.
>
> ~Lauraan Marron (age 9)

structure and to the homes that lay below. By eleven o'clock, David decided it was time. He called Chris, and they began evacuations in the vicinity of Cooper Hill. "I stayed there," remembers David, "and Michael [Kercewich] stayed there, and we monitored the water from Cooper Hill." From that point until the early morning, Kim remembers, someone was always watching the culvert.

"So Chris went out knocking on doors," Kim recalls, "but only those that looked to be in immediate danger." As the night wore on, the list kept growing. At about 11:00 he came to Jack and Hazel Fuller's horse farm on Spooner Flats just above Cooper Hill. "They were very surprised to see me," he remembers, "but very pleasant." He warned them of the danger, but didn't urge them to leave. "Hazel has her whole life wrapped up in her horses… If I had told them to leave their farm and their horses had perished, I would have a hard time living with myself."

The water was already coming into the garage of another house by the river. "'What should we do?" the couple asked, and Chris advised them to bring all their financial materials with them. Several minutes later they came out clinging to three bags of possessions and drove off into the night—to friends? To relatives? There wasn't time to ask or wonder. Chris called his wife at this point, told her he had no idea when he was coming home, and hurried to the police station to call in his secretary and lieutenant. Since he had become the town's police chief, he had prepared for something like this—a blizzard or an ice storm— stocking the station with equipment, a generator, and recently with a gift from the Fullers: two UHF radios. He had bought antennas and had the radios installed: "It might have cost the town three hundred dollars," he said afterwards, "the best three hundred dollars ever spent."

While he was at the police station Lieutenant Bob Bromley modified an old base radio so that the road agent and police chief could communicate with the station throughout the night.

Kitty Kmiec could hear the events unfolding from her house at 20 Forest Road near the intersection with Griffin Hill Road.

> I never slept that night. I listened to the scanner all night long, because I knew we were in a state of emergency. I could hear Kim Kercewich, the fire chief…He had set up station down at the police station, and he

monitored all night long and he kept checking, and they had someone stationed at the Lake Warren Dam, somebody stationed at Cooper Hill, and then David Crosby was driving the roads to check the conditions, so that if any roads were not passable he could post them…and Chief Lyons, we could hear him all night long, and all night long they kept in touch with each other.

Back on the road, Chris Lyons asked his friend John Anderson to keep a log of all the houses at which they stopped. Anticipating trouble, he told John to flag all the houses where no one came to the door so that they could return to these houses later in the night if conditions grew worse. At the same time, Lieutenant Bromley was working at the station, transferring all the information with grease pens onto a town map covered with Plexiglas. He marked in homes that were in trouble, indicated washed out roads, and recorded all other critical information with different colors and symbols. Secretary Michelle Koson worked with him on the phone, making follow-up calls to citizens who wouldn't open their doors. Despite the sudden nature of their work, Chief Lyons would say afterwards, "We had a good grip on what was going on in the town."

Sunday Morning

Nine-year old Lauraann Marron was upstairs playing with her toy puma when she and her family were evacuated from their house on Forest Road at the foot of Hatch Hill. "When I was little I always wanted to make a boat, like in that story, like God did it…when I was little, I planned it." Instead she drove with her parents to the safety of a hotel.

At about midnight, Chief Lyons, had decided to open the fire station/town hall to evacuees, and Anton Elbers helped set it up:

> We were starting to try to pull together supplies for people who had been evacuated. There really hadn't been any preparation ahead of time, so just finding cots—there were no cots—trying to find mattresses or mats…There were people who had brought their dogs and cats…and there was no place [for anyone] to lie down. This was about 12:00 or 1:00 at night. We were trying to make do with stuff we had. Most people there were too much in shock to even try to lie down; most people were just sitting and talking.

From Alstead Emergency Operations Center and Keene Mutal Aid log.s:

23:45

Notified selectmen & Linda Christie [administrative assistant]

01:14 A.M.

Activating Lake Warren Dam Emergency Plan

02:36

Lyons advises residents along Route 123 from Cooper Hill to Route 12A to evacuate. Some are leaving. Others have refused to vacate.

Soon supplies poured in—pillows, blankets, mats, and big bread carriers tipped upside down to raise the mats off the floor. Firefighter Donna Olmstead ran home and grabbed whatever she could, pulling food from her refrigerator to stock the station and try to make people comfortable. Mary Lou Huffling brought sleeping bags and cots. Yet despite their best efforts to make people comfortable, residents were anxious. "Nobody slept well all night," remembers Mary Lou. Seven-year-old Dylan Martin might have been the exception. As he slept on a makeshift bed he remembers, "There were nice candles on top of the table that kept me warm."

In East Alstead, Eleanor Elber's house became its own kind of retreat. When Courtney Porter heard that her friends couldn't get through to pick her up, she drove her borrowed car to the Orchard Hill Farm to spend the night. Eleanor's friends from Seattle, meanwhile, were still on the road. "Eleanor was on the phone trying to talk these guys through how to get back here." Courtney remembers, "And they went some crazy route through Keene." Even with guidance, Eleanor recollects, "It took them three hours…and it wasn't because they got lost; it was because they hit one huge amount of dark water after another."

Few people could sleep that night. By now Kitty Kmiec was in bed, but she still couldn't take her attention off her scanner and the drama unfolding up and down the river. Matt Goodell eventually put his children to bed, but he stayed up: "I couldn't sleep if I wanted to because the sound of the boulders was literally shaking the house." Matt Saxton, now at his friend's house in Gilsum, was far from the rising water, but he couldn't take his mind off of it. "I didn't sleep in Gilsum. I went to bed in Gilsum, but I didn't sleep."

2:00 A.M.

Anton Elbers walked from the Alstead Village fire station to the police station. "I heard this boom, boom, boom…it took me a little while to realize it wasn't thunder: it was boulders being carried down the river." The river was high when he walked into the police station, but when he came out fifteen minutes later, it had overflowed its banks, flooding the parking lot. "That whole area was underwater, and it was like, whoa!" Vehicles were quickly moved to higher ground, but the water receded. "It was the sign of things to come," Anton observed. It was only 2:30, and the rain kept falling.

Christopher Lyons's situation was becoming desperate. Although he was on the phone with the New Hampshire Office of Emergency Management throughout the night, high water troubles had begun seventeen miles away in Keene, and he knew that any aid would gravitate to the larger city. Moreover, resources were meager:

We only have one cruiser. We can't ask for help from the neighboring towns because Walpole was experiencing problems. I remember there was a Walpole officer needing help, but we couldn't go to him because we had our own problems. It's one of those things where you get twisted in about fifty different directions; you want to be helpful to your neighbors that help you, but we can't help each other. You know the old saying, you can't get there from here? You really couldn't get there…I was getting limited to where I could go…And everybody's using all that they could.

By this time many roads were already closed, and others were fast becoming impassable. Alstead and East Alstead were already split by the currents. Thinking ahead to the chaos that would ensue the following morning, Chief Lyons found time to write an announcement for the local radio stations, saying in effect: Please stay away. Don't come here.

It was nearing three o'clock in the morning when things began to change. "The water had all stabilized," David Crosby remembers, "Everything had come up, and it was just sitting there. It had pretty much stopped raining." Lark Leonard was lying awake in East Alstead at the time, and she heard the squirrels begin to play with acorns on the roof. "I listened to them rolling around and I thought, *Great, the rain has stopped.*" But the sense of relief was short-lived. The rain began afresh and the water continued to rise, recalls David. "That's when we really decided we'd better get everybody out of everywhere we can get them from."

3:00 A.M.

"Evacuating people is not an easy thing," Chief Lyons later explained.

> People say, 'Oh…it's just…you go banging on doors and people wake up and they go running out the door.'
>
> It doesn't happen that way. Because I don't know how many people on [Route] 123 had a lot of different situations. They had medical issues. There were two or three homes with people on oxygen tanks—I mean, they are on [oxygen] all the time; they have to have it with them. You just don't tell somebody, and they run out to their vehicles. There were people that we engaged in conversation with who said, 'Hey, it ain't goin' to be that bad,' and there were people who were blowing us down.

03:00

Water level stabilizes at Cooper Hill culvert

04:31

South side of Lake Warren dam is eroding. Emergency personnel at East Alstead Fire Station are monitoring the dam.

Sometimes it was difficult to simply get people to their doors. "Hearing that night was hard for everyone," Chief Lyons remembers. The combination of rain and rushing water muffled shouting, knocking and, in some cases, even his sirens. If the door was unlocked they would open it and shout. But some doors were locked, and many people were not eager to open their doors so early in the morning. Eleven-year-old Angela Hilow was sleeping when she heard knocking on her door. "My mom said later that it was a police officer. He didn't have his lights on, so my mom wasn't going to answer the door because she didn't know who it was."

Chief Lyons was not surprised by this:

> There's a reason why some of those people didn't answer the door. You pounded on the door; and you think about kicking doors in, but that's a dangerous thing to do. How many people in this town have guns? And you know what? That's why they have them, because if someone busted in their door—and they're not going to know it's me—they're not going to mean to shoot me, but they are going to shoot me, because they'll be in fear of their life.
>
> There's a lot of people who criticize me for not kicking doors in, but, like I said, I'm not going to go kicking doors in for two reasons. Number one, the safety factor: for my safety. And number two, I would be the biggest idiot if I went and kicked twelve doors in, and then nothing happened. I would have overreacted. So those two things sat in the back of my head.

Each delay, however, meant the neighbors had to wait. Chris knew that one particular couple had a scanner in their house, but they took a long time to answer the door. "Those were the things that really hurt."

Of course then there was the task of convincing people to leave. "I'm soaking wet, and I'm trying to tell them that this is serious." But many people would not take his word for it. "We told them that they should leave, that things weren't looking real good, but there was no way of forcing them," remembers Kim Kercewich. "That was one of the things that the police chief was quite discouraged over—that a lot of the people who had lived here for a long time basically told him, 'You don't know what you're talking about. We've lived here our whole life. This is nothing new.' And so there were people who flat out refused to leave."

Sometimes it required a more personal touch. When the mother-of-a-friend of Angela Hilow's sister called later in the morning, the family decided to evacuate. Farther up the river, Scott Gendron refused to leave until David Crosby asked secretary Michelle Koson to deliver a personal message: "I said to get the hell out! And if [we] hadn't called Scott and told him to get out, he would have stayed there."

Chief Lyons also did his best. Although there was no response when he knocked on Vera LaFluer's door, he had a feeling she was there. After Michelle tried calling her in vain, he returned with all his sirens blaring. Finally she woke up—only to have an asthma attack as they were leaving. "It doesn't help the situation," Chris remembers, "You know, I wasn't mean to Vera, but the neighbor next door needed to be told [to evacuate]. So all this time that I'm losing, that I've lost—it's not that I'm angry, but in a situation like that, you have to get people moving. That was my job: to get people to move whether they like it or not." So he said, "Vera, I'm sorry, but you have to get a hold of yourself…do you have an inhaler?" Vera did pull herself together enough to take her pets to dry ground.

Packing, of course, was another complication for many. In the face of so much uncertainty, what should they take? The pets? The photo album? Identification? Resident Bobbie Wilson's husband had always teased her, that if she were evacuated, she would pack the whole china cabinet. But she took the church checkbook, the ambulance checkbooks, and the tractor keys. A little way up the road—just below the Cooper Hill culvert—Sharon Perry recounted her own dilemma:

> I was getting ready to leave, putting some things in a suitcase, because I knew we'd have to. I was kind of assessing what I should take with me and what I should leave there, and there were so many things I thought of—like my bride doll. It was up on a dresser, and I thought… I'd had her since I was ten. She was old, and she had her original clothes and everything. And she was up on a dresser, and I almost took her, and then I thought, That's silly!—
>
> I can't take her and not take Ernie's guns. And they were all up higher, so I thought they'd all be okay next day. So what I did take—I took the photograph album. I knew I had our birth certificates and our marriage license, and my passport. I got a passport when my son went to Iraq, just in case I needed it. He's going again, so I'm glad that I took that (nothing's going to happen to him, though). And I took one picture of my boys when they were little, and I took my parent's wedding picture off the wall. And I don't know why I took those things. I just did.

05:30

No change in condition of Lake Warren Dam. Water level behind Cooper Hill culvert is within 2 feet of the road surface.

Sometimes residents were not ready to pack up in the middle of the night, as the fire chief observed. "I mean they ran into that all the time: 'Yah…don't worry about it…we're all set. Go away. Leave us alone.'" When Bobbie Wilson, a member of the rescue squad, began evacuating her neighbors, she ran into this more than once. At one home, a woman had a two-month-old baby and a husband who said there was nothing to worry about. "I grabbed her, pulled her out into the rain, and took her out to show her how tall the water was. I am a mother, and I said, 'You are putting your children at risk!" But the family stayed until early the next morning.

Maggie Gacek, who also didn't leave her house until the following morning, remembers the logic behind her decision:

> Some time in the middle of the night, two or three o'clock in the morning, the police chief came to the door. Apparently, he came twice. The first time he couldn't get us up. I came back downstairs. Mom—Stella Winham—came downstairs, and he said, "You better get your stuff and get out."
> And Mom said, "No," and went back to bed…I was getting really nervous… You could hear this BANG, BANG, BANG, BANG, which—I didn't know what it was. I assumed it was rocks hitting Bobbie Wilson's bridge… So this is the stupid theory: The rocks are hitting the bridge. The bridge is still there. There is no flood. There is no danger.…That's the logic. That's the logic I had when the police chief came around three o'clock. Yeah, we went back upstairs.

As frustrated as he was with residents' refusals to leave, David Crosby sympathizes, "I know darn well, if I wasn't in the position I was, and living where I was, and they came knocking on my door, I'd have said just like everyone else, "What are you nuts? I ain't leaving."

Yet the hardest part, Chris remembers, was not the outright refusals, but the refusals that took a lot of time. With many residents expressing their fears as anger, this was not an uncommon problem. "Some of these people were very standoffish, very, very nasty. I don't understand, I'm sorry…but at least they could have said, 'I feel like I'm okay. Thank you for telling me that.' Or else give me an answer [so] that I'm not going to…keep trying to explain on and on and on to the point where it's getting ridiculous!" Toward the end, he began to learn how to spend less time: he stressed the severity of the situation and let people make their own decisions. Yet these decisions often mystified him, "I still, to this day, am totally baffled as to how people acted how they did, because in the three and a half years that I've served this town, I never gave a false alarm."

5:00 A.M.

The fire personnel, ambulance crew, police force, selectmen, and volunteers had been up all night. "We were maxxed out. Everyone who could possibly work was working," Chief Lyons recalls. Yet there was one more person he could call in. "That morning, exactly at 4:56, Chief Lyons called to ask me to come in to make coffee and open early for people," remembers Delvina Kearney, the new owner of the Alstead Village Market. "I felt that if it was that important to him to call me to come in…I got up and got going."

David Crosby, meanwhile, pulled Chris up to Cooper Hill, where a lake's worth of water was now collecting on Spooner Flats, forcing its way through the twelve-foot culvert.

> There were whirlpools up there that you could take a town truck…a one-ton town truck…and hold it, and stick it down inside that whirlpool and you wouldn't get it wet. That's how big they were. And there was white foam and stuff going down into this whirlpool, just the culvert sucking the air, trying to get the water through.

When the water came out the other end, Mike Kercewich remembers, it was forced out and up in a long stream with the same cork-screw patterning as the lining of the culvert. David brought Chris over to see this spectacle. "Chris," he said, "this whole thing is going to go."

Alstead Village Market. *Photograph by Jeanne Moody*

05:38

Crosby requests evacuation notification below Cooper Hill. Water 2 feet from cresting road.

05:45

Water up to grasss on Cooper Hill Road

05:53

Tree down on Hill Road above Comstock Road

06:07

Water level dropping at Lake Warren dam

The longer he watched, the more certain David became:

> It was holding, everything was holding fine because the back side of it was all riprapped with ledge, but the water got so deep that it started coming down the state road on the inside of the turn. And when it did, it couldn't quite get over the bump in the tar so that shoved it off between Cooper Hill and this road out here…There was a bunch of mailboxes there. The water just started running off; it made a little tiny wormhole and just kept growing and growing and growing and growing…it ate itself right back underneath the rocks. So it took all the dirt out from underneath the rocks and let the rocks drop in. The water was just running water on dirt, and everything was going…When we first saw the little wormhole, that was when we first started evacuating River Street.

06:08

Water over Cooper Hill Road

Now David joined in the evacuations himself and began to experience what the others had gone through all night. "When we went down on River Street, getting people off…they came to the door, madder than hell: 'Quit beating on my door! What the hell you doing?' And they were nasty, they were nasty—a lot of them…Some of them were like, 'Okay, we're gone.'"

Anton Elbers was also helping with the evacuations, working up from just below the gun shop on lower River Street to the village. At one house, he evacuated a couple who had recently moved to Alstead from Florida to escape the hurricanes. "I felt bad for them," Anton remembers. A little way up the road he evacuated an elderly couple—Marlene and Leroy Wade. It was not even six o'clock, and their house was already shaking. As he wheeled Leroy out on his wheelchair, Marlene remembered something.

"I have to get my purse…It's out back."

"You don't want to go there," one of the rescue workers said and hurried them to the fire station. The back of their house was hanging over the river.

6:00 A.M.

"Around six or so," Mary Lou Huffling remembers, "some of the rescue workers came and said that we needed to evacuate the fire station and move to higher ground." The people within began moving their vehicles or simply walking up Hill Road. "There was no destination—just to get out. This precipitated a new level of anxiety."

In her home, however, Kitty Kmiec was not too concerned about her own safety, as there was a ten-foot rise between her house and the river. "It had quite a bit it had to fill before it would overflow." That morning, however, she had overheard David Crosby's concern on the scanner:

> I think it was about six o'clock: I heard David, and he said, 'I think it's at the top of Cooper Hill, just a couple inches from the top,' and shortly after that I heard him say, 'It's coming over the top and its faster and stronger than I expected.' And shortly after that…'It's starting to erode by the mailboxes; it's going to go; I'm getting out of here!' And that's when I got up, and got the kids up, and got a couple pairs of outfits together and grabbed some food.

Her brother-in-law who worked for the North Walpole Fire Department advised them to leave, but they were so far from the river, so much higher than the river, they decided to see what would happen.

It was about quarter past six when Tom W. Hancock woke up and got dressed. "I could already hear the water—it sounded like Niagara Falls coming over Cooper Hill…just a noise that… *oh, that noise isn't supposed to be there.*" When he went out to investigate, he saw that the guard rails that had stretched up the side of Cooper Hill had been undermined, and were hanging in the water, pulled taut by the force of the current. "They were humming. If you were to take a guitar string and run water over it, that's the noise the guard rails were making."

David Crosby took another trip up the river to check on the culvert and found considerably more water than he had left. "There was an awful surge of water that came above that. There was more water in there—half again as much—as in all Lake Warren." John Fuller's horse farm was transformed:

> We got up, and there was a message…from Michelle at the police station asking if we were all right, just checking on our status and wondering how things were going, so before I called back down there I grabbed a dressing gown and a flashlight and went back outside and looked around, and I was just flabbergasted. It was raining hard again, and there was just a gigantic lake below us, between here and Cooper Hill. All we could see was water and debris floating on the water…The smell was horrendous…all you could smell was fuel oil.

06:10

Code Red for Cooper Hill. Martin and Lyons beginning evacuations. Martin River Street Lyons Cooper Hill on down

06:15

Code Red on Lake Warren Dam

06:30

Water cresting over Cooper Hill. Not looking good.

06:55

Mutual Aid was asked to notify Langdon & Walpole about possibility of sudden surge.

07:00

Cooper Hill culvert has let loose.

07:25

"All hell broke loose."

Downstream, Anton had worked most of the way up River Street, but he was hearing reports from Cooper Hill and knew that time was running out: *Okay, we're going along here and if it starts going, how far do we have to run to get up the hill?* He was eyeing the river bank as he went. "I had no idea how long it would take for that water to get down from Cooper Hill, down to town."

Delvina Kearney, meanwhile, had made it across the Drewsville Bridge into Alstead and was in the store putting on a pot of coffee. When Scott Gendron came in at about ten minutes to seven, Delvina remembers the lights beginning to flicker. "And I said, 'Something really bad is happening.' You could look out the door and see the water across the street just rising and rising. It was like little tidal waves getting bigger and bigger and bigger…"

7:00 A.M.

Almut Yakovleff had woken up earlier in the morning, but because it was Sunday she had decided to go back to sleep. At seven o'clock she received a phone call telling her to evacuate. "I remember I had a very hard time putting on my socks. I was shaking, and I realized I wasn't going to run out of the house without socks on my feet." Farther up the river, Angela Hilow was packing. "We took my sister's hamster, my mom's cat and my rabbit…When we were driving up the hill, my mom could see water coming up the back of our yard…"

A crowd was gathering in the village. "I remember there were a lot of people standing," said Chief Lyons, "I told them to get back, and they told me I was overreacting…It was crazy: people were just not obeying us!"

Despite his warnings, a daring boy sprinted across the bridge. "The water was just shy of going over that bridge anyhow…I said, 'If this bridge doesn't go I'll be surprised.' And the boy turned around, about to run over again. John [Anderson] says, "Don't you do it!" and the boy says, "I can run fast." But something made him change his mind.

Shortly After 7:00 A.M.

Matt Saxton was on the phone:

> I called my mother, and I asked, "So what's going on over there?"
> And she said, "Well, it's raining, and it's just awful." She stopped what she was saying a little after seven o'clock, and then she said, "I am watching the bottom of Cooper Hill wash completely away."

The Flood

> *The Cold River went on a wild rampage through Alstead.*
>
> *~ Bradley Gordon (age 11)*

Overleaf: Rising waters of Warren Brook on the evening of Oct. 8. *Photograph by Carl Babbitt*

With the rising water now almost touching his barn, John Fuller and his wife Hazel decided to relocate the bailer that was stored inside.

> I jumped off the tractor into the puddle…and as I walked around the front of the tractor, the puddle disappeared from under my feet. I looked up, and everything that was floating out in our hayfield just took off, all headed down towards town. We just looked at each other; our faces just dropped. We were horrified. We ran for the house—for the phone, but we knew what had happened, that it was too late.
>
> *John Fuller*

Less than half a mile downstream, Cooper Hill Road and its culvert, which had strained to bear an endless deluge of water, rain, and debris, had collapsed.

> The noise was just incredible: splintering, gushing water. The trees were actually being broken like toothpicks. Just take a sixteen- to eighteen-inch diameter cane and break it over your knee: it's the sound of it. The ground was shaking.
>
> *Thomas W. Hancock*

Spooner Flats looking south from the Sherwood house about ten minutes after the Cooper Hill Road culvert broke about a half mile to the west (right). The swash line on the shed in the foreground shows the high water mark of the flood. *Photograph by Gregory Sherwood*

I looked up ahead of me, and the first thing that came to mind was that the dam at Lake Warren had broken, because there was a wall of water coming at me. At this point I stopped and I said, *Oh my gosh! I need to get out of here!* Because it was coming at me. It was probably about 150 yards away from me. And the wall of water was probably 12 to 15 feet high. I put the car in reverse and backed down. I couldn't turn into the [nearest] driveway because I was already a little below it. And I said there's got to be another driveway on the right side going down so I can get up the hill to get away from this thing.

Jean Vaillancourt

The location of the Cooper Hill Road Culvert with the west end of Spooner Flats in the background. The broken end of Cooper Hill Road is on the right. Guard rail posts on Forest Road (Rte. 123) are shown in the upper left. *Photograph by Steve Fortier*

My wife got on the radio and hollered, 'The trees are snapping off, there's stuff coming down through, and there are trailers jumping up in the air across the road!' At that time, I could see the water coming, so I spun my truck around in the road, and I went to right behind where Bill Seale was, behind Griffin Hill; there's a trailer there. There was a woman, a man, and two or three kids there that didn't leave, so I stopped there, and I had a hell of a time getting them out of there. They just were not going to go!

Finally I got really angry, and they decided they'd better go, but they just kept on wanting to go back in the house and put stuff in the car, and I said, 'You don't have time! Get!' At this time I could look up by Rock Wilson's and see the water coming at me. So they finally got out of there and went up [Route] 12A, and I stopped at Bill Seale's because he was outside, and I told him, 'Bill, you've got to leave, and you've got to leave now!' And he was not going to leave. And I said, 'Bill, look behind you.' Water was just coming everywhere. It was just as dry as this floor when I walked to his house, and I wasn't there thirty seconds and the water was up to my knees.

It started like it was pushing way out ahead of it to start with, and behind it was just a big wall of water with trees and mobile homes just bubbling on… It was like somebody surfing, that's what it looked like. And then when it smashed into things… When I left Bill Seale, he was walking rapidly up 12A. How he got to be where he did [afterwards], I don't have a clue. The water was hitting on the back of my truck. That's why I didn't put him in my truck, because I didn't know whether I was going swimming or not.

David Crosby

The flood wave hits the Walier's garden shed on the banks of the Cold River on River Street (Route 123).
Photograph by Todd Walier

Evacuation
by Matt Goodell

At a quarter to seven, I crawled into bed. And literally ten to fifteen minutes later they started kicking the doors in. They were slamming on the house, and I went to the door thinking it was my neighbor wanting one of the pumps back. It ends up being a fire official telling us we got to get out. I was like:

"What do you mean, we've got to get out?" because when I looked out, the water—in that short period—had actually receded back, so we're thinking, *Why are we getting out?*

He looked at me and he said that the culvert had dammed up the water and had just burst, and we had literally minutes to get out, or we'd all be dead. So I said, "Okay."

He left. My wife came out and I said, "Get the kids up, and we've got to get out." And I didn't want to freak everybody out, so I was trying to keep to myself what was going on, even though she kept kind of asking questions. And she got the kids up, and I was throwing some stuff in the car, getting out animals—we have a dog and a cat—I was throwing them in the crate and loading them into the car. And as the kids went out, she was coming out to get in the car, and I stopped her in the doorway and said,

"If you've got one possession you can grab in three seconds, grab it now." And that's when she kind of freaked out a little bit on me. And she—you know, panic situation—she couldn't think of anything. So she just went straight out to the car.

I went in to grab my jacket and opened up the closet, and there was a family picture that we still hadn't hung—one of those things. I grabbed the picture; I didn't have time to think. I grabbed that; threw that in the car. And Scott Gendron was actually driving by, and he said—because I had my Harley in the driveway—he said, "What are you doing with that bike?"

And I said, "Leaving it here. I mean, what am I going to do with it?"

He said, "Throw it up at my shop when you go by on the way to the fire station."

And I said, "Okay." My wife drove, and I followed her up on my bike. And I threw the bike in front of the garage [Citgo gas station], and we went to the fire station where they told us to go, and that was about seven o'clock.

I saw a whole bunch of water coming down the river bed, and appliances like refrigerators and so forth floating by… rushing by, and cars nose down, sticking straight up into the air, crashing into trees—all kinds of debris, just flying down the river. I grabbed a camera. I took a few pictures, and by the time I had taken four pictures…the water had come up over the road, and was coming up near the driveway. We have a two- or three-foot rise from the road up to our lawn, and it was coming up near the top of the lawn. Then I noticed the phone poles were cracking and starting to fall down and coming towards our house, so I went back in the house. I wasn't outside anymore.

Downed telephone pole near the Larsen place on Forest Road (Rte. 123). The collapsed Sheldon place (Bellows or Thompson place) is in the background. *Photograph by Stacy Eaton.*

One of the last things I saw before I came back into the house was this big, huge black object coming down the river. It looked like a tremendous black bladder or something. I couldn't comprehend what it might be, and it ended up it was the culvert from underneath Cooper Hill Road. The culvert's about twelve feet in diameter and fifty feet long. And that was floating down front in the park right across the street in front of our house.

Robert Larsen

The other thing was the noise, and it wasn't just the rush of the water. I thought it was a cannon going off, but that made no sense. It was boulders hitting boulders as they went downstream.

Mary Larsen

Part of the 12-foot diameter Cooper Hill Road culvert that came to rest in front of the Larsen's house about 0.6 miles downstream from Forristall Corners. *Photograph by Robert Larsen.*

You hear about floods and hurricanes in other places, but you never think about it happening in your own small town.

~Marie Simoneaux (age 11)

The houses didn't actually float, they just disintegrated. Like the water came in on the upper level of the house, and the pressure just broke the houses apart. Right where they were standing, they just broke apart. Whole sections of [a house] would just blow off. You know, the windows, the water was shooting out the windows. It was something that I had never seen before.

Jean Vaillancourt

At shortly after seven in the morning, when we got to Kmiec's corner, we saw the wall of water coming at us. We were that close to it. We were within two hundred feet of it. It was very scary. It was probably fifteen, twenty feet high, and we could see the trees and the debris, and this bottom of a truck, just going end for end in front of us.

Meredith Howard

We woke up and all we heard was this thunderous roaring and we didn't know what it was. We thought our air conditioner had broken.

Derek Sherburne

Debris from destroyed buildings upstream (right) caught by a guardrail on the Griffin Hill Road Bridge across Warren Brook. *Photograph by Mike Heidorn*

So, I actually remember standing up from my bed and beating on the air conditioner. I figured that was what was going on. I'd never heard the river that loud.

Jesse Sherburne

Then the telephone pole out in our yard… the wire started to sway, and then the whole pole started to sway, and I thought it was going to actually fall over and land on the car… and then we could hear it coming. We could hear the trees snapping, and popping, and cracking as they were all coming down, and you could even see it. You could see the trees fall, and then all of a sudden it came around the corner, and it was just this great big mass of brown wall of mud and water and whatever coming right down the brook bed. I jumped in the car and took off, and [Brad] jumped in the truck with my son, and they came behind me.

Kitty Kmiec

Flood waters cascade off the north end of Mechanic Street just above the ledge at the Wooden Dam area.
Photograph by Dale Dustin

Flood debris in a bend of the Cold River at the east end of Mechanic Street (Routes 12A and 123) above the ledge (site of former Wooden Dam) and just below the mouth of Warren Brook,. *Photograph courtesy of the New Hampshire Department of Safety*

Flood
by Meghan Hilow, age 11

One really, really early October morning, destruction hit a small town by the name of Alstead. Roads and houses were destroyed. Some people died. Much sadness came to many families. Many people lost things they held dear, including me. My house was destroyed in the flood. This is my terrible story.

Early in the morning on October 9, 2005, the police started knocking on people's doors, trying to warn them of what they thought could happen. When they knocked on our door, my mom didn't answer it. It was about 3:00 A.M. and the person did not identify themselves or have any lights flashing. After knocking only once, they got back in their vehicle and left. My mom went back to sleep.

At 6:00 a.m, my friend Jacadi Simard called my house, woke my mom up, and told her the Cold River was going to flood. The river [Warren Brook] runs through our backyard, and we could be in danger. After talking to Jacadi's mom, my mom woke us quickly and told us we had to go. We grabbed clothes for just a couple days and took our animals out to the car. We just thought it was something minor since our house was far away from the river, and we didn't understand what was really going on. I think my mom realized it was very serious when the police and another man showed up at about 7:00 a.m and told us to leave immediately, because the dam was going to break at any moment. We ran to the car with my mom's cat Pooky. We had a hard time catching her. She was very scared. When we left the driveway, a guy was yelling the dam had broken. As we turned to go up the hill to Jacadi's house, we saw water start to go down our backyard. We were all very scared. I found out after that our house was washed away not five minutes after we had left.

After a couple of hours, my step dad went down to see if everything was okay. When he returned, he said everything was gone. My mom and I immediately went down to see if it was true. I was shocked by what I saw. My mom started crying. I couldn't cry. We went back to Jacadi's house and told my sister, Angela, and the rest of them that everything was gone. Jacadi and I both started to cry when we told her.

Later, we all went down to see the destruction. During my second trip, I didn't just notice that my house was gone, I noticed all the damage that had been done. A lot of homes were gone, roads destroyed, trees were uprooted, and a lot more damage was done. People's lives were thrown apart and several people died, including my neighbor, Bill Seale.

Around 4:00 p.m,, we went to my Great-Grandmother Rosemary's house to stay for a while. This was a very devastating thing that happened. I have to say that after the flood, I was sad and depressed, and I'm probably still a little depressed. Right now, all I can do is write.

We watched [the water] come down the end of the pond, and we watched it come through here, taking trees down, terribly noisy. We watched it take out the snowmobile bridge here. We watched [the bridge] jump up and down, up and down, and then finally it went…There were three cars right in front of the garage there. They were parked in a line out towards the bridge, and instantly the water came out from under those cars and higher-pressure…just blew it. Then the cars came sideways and we slowly drove around the corner. At that point we drove beside [the flood surge] and watched it go down taking trees. Telephone poles are going back and forth and they're actually slapping, the wires slapping each other.

Brad Kmiec

Vilas Pool Dam the morning of the flood. *Photograph by David Collins.*

I was in the police station, standing there in the door, looking out, and I could see [David Crosby] coming down Mechanic Street, and I'd look up the green and… nothing there yet. And I watched him come all the way down through and go behind the town office.

And then that chain link fence that was up there, the water started to come through that, and I'm standing there looking at that, saying to myself, Oh, that doesn't look too bad. This ain't gonna be bad. This ain't bad… Michelle, it's time to go!

Michelle Koson is a police secretary. She was down there helping run the police side of the radios and keeping track of all the calls and everything that was going on.

 She said 'Just a minute.'

'We've got to go now.'

'Just a minute, I've got a little more to do.'

'Michelle! We have to go now!'

'Okay! Oops, I forgot my pocketbook.'

I'd already checked earlier just in case we did have to leave, and we couldn't get out the back door. We'd go up the steps to the town selectman's office. There's a hollow-core door up there, and I knew that I could get through that if I had to. She finally came out of the office, and I started to go up the stairs. 'Oh, we can't go that way. It's locked.'

I turned around and looked at her, and I could look out that back door of the police station through glass, and the water was starting to lap on that yellow stripe in the parking lot. And I think what happened was she turned around and looked too, and she said 'Okay.' And up the stairs we went and broke the door through, and we went in and tried to break the next door until I remembered it was unlocked from the inside. Out the door we went. Got out in front of the town office, and [David Crosby had] parked on the low side. Michelle went over and got in his truck. I had moved my pickup earlier. I went and got in that and started to back out. Then I stopped and looked across the green, and I had to pull back into the parking lot. Five hundred-gallon propane tanks were just rolling down across the green, and every time they'd roll over you'd see the propane vapor, the white vapor, squirting out.

Kim Kercewich

> *You don't know what you have until it's gone.*
>
> *~Lauren Ramsey (age 11)*

My dad's old truck ended up in the yard of the person he bought it from.

~Mollie Gendron (age 11)

There was a mobile home that I watched come right down through, it stayed right in the river channel. It was all together, like nothing had ever happened to it. It was just floating, and when it smacked the [Alstead Village] bridge, it just disintegrated. It never came out the other end, just a whole bunch of little pieces, and off it went. [Then came] Rock Wilson's outside wood furnace, just floating down the brook, smoke coming out.

David Crosby

I don't know how high [the water] was, maybe sixteen feet, coming towards us…I thought it was going to hit us; I thought that was it. Nobody was moving; everybody was in shock. As I was looking out on the Cold River you could see animals, pieces of houses… It sounded like the ocean, like rushing water, like the tide flowing in. I was so scared and so shaken that I think my senses weren't functioning. You know, I've been through an earthquake… I felt as jittery and shaking as after a very powerful earthquake. It's like your hearing gets dulled; your senses get dulled. When I looked at that wall of water I wasn't running; I had no feet; I had no motion in my body. That thing just swept me away.

Daniel Higgins

[Debris] would be on the surface of the water and then another piece would be… it looked like big boulders. It was going frighteningly fast and then

Water rushes over March Hill Road in Walpole near Alstead town line. *Photograph by Nicholas Brown*

I realized that the power of this river is phenomenal: it's just one angry, raging river that's able to take just anything and everything.

Almut Yakovleff

I heard people scream that the water was coming, and so I turned around and walked over towards the library. You could see that the water was starting to flood over the Millot Green. It was very quick from there to where it was flooding over the bridge. And we were watching cars…I remember this red car bobbing along, just bobbing along. There was a point where the water was coming over the top of the bridge and flooding around. It was like four feet deep in the street there…and there was so much debris in the river, I mean it was hard to see the water there was so much construction debris, gas tanks… There was a thousand-gallon gas tank that came floating along the top of the water and that was scary thinking about: what if those hit something and decided to blow up?

Anton Elbers

While we were at the fire department we looked out, and they told us we had to get out…There was this wall of water that came right over the top of the bridge, and with it was this little red pickup truck. I'll never forget it. And it was just floating around, and it ended up in front of the library. But when the wall of water came over, that must have been when it took my home, because shortly after that, they told me that my home was gone. That the river had taken my home.

Marlene Wade

Cold River near Wooden Dam just east of Vilas School as water recedes. *Photograph by Charlie Brady*

The water… looked like chocolate milk.

~Lyle Doolittle (age 12)

Flood waters surge across Millot Green.
Video image by Donalin Ring

Flood surge takes out trees along bank of the Cold River. The basketball hoop indicates the depth of the water.
Video image by Donalin Ring

Flood waters inundate the police station in the Municipal Building on Millot Green. *Photograph by David Collins*

Waters flood the center of Alstead Village.
Photograph by David Collins

Journey of the cook shack from Millot Green across Alstead Village Bridge. *Photographer unknown*

Waters rushes over Alstead Village Bridge immediately after flood peak. *Photograph by Steve Fortier*

The journey of the red truck across Alstead Village to the library lawn. *Photographer unknown.*   *Photograph by Steve Fortier*

Journey from Gilsum to Alstead

From an interview with Matt Saxton

[My friends in Gilsum] loaned me a pair of Sorel boots. We got in the jeep, and we got to the bottom of Corbin Road and Thayer Brook Road. Essentially, now Thayer Brook Road was Thayer Brook, so they let me out and looked rather dubious what I was going to try to do, which was to get to the town hall. I said don't worry about me. I'll go through the back woods if I have to. It'll be fine.

So off they went to Keene and I jumped the water running beside Corbin Road and went into the woods and went through the woods until I saw a place on Thayer Brook Road where it was dry enough, so I jumped the water and got on it, and I found Junior and Amy Buffum, each with a shovel, standing in the road looking bewildered. They said that they thought that they were going to be able to help, but it was going to take more than them with the shovels. I guess that was right.

As I was standing there talking, a pickup truck with two young men in it roared around the corner and drove through the water in the road, and then stopped. I said "Where are you headed?" They were trying to get west, but they weren't having any luck, and I said I'm trying to head west and not having any luck. They said to hop in, so I hopped into the truck with the two young men, who were a lot more daring than anyone else I had met all day. They got me just down the hill from here, just by Nancy's next door, where the road was half gone and the part that was gone was full of rushing water. I said I could walk the rest of the way, thanks. They turned around, and I don't know what happened to them after that. Anyway, I walked up the hill and got home and changed into more appropriate clothing. I got in my van and I decided I would drive south until I couldn't anymore, and that turned out to be the Clark farm, not more than a mile and a half from here, but more than a mile from where the culvert had washed out. So I left my van in the middle of the road, knowing it would not be in the way, and waded through water and jumped the ditch. I got down to my mother, who was living at the time in the house just above the culvert. "So," I asked, "how bad is it?" There were no words. "You have to see this yourself," she said. We talked for a minute longer, then I set off on foot to get to the town office. I got… well, it was just horrifying.

I got down to the flood valley, and Larry's house was gone. It was just staggering. There was not really a way to describe it. The whole upper end of the culvert was just gone. There was a lot of water around. The culvert had been utterly destroyed. You'd walk along on pavement, then jump down where there wasn't any pavement for six or seven feet, and then clamber up again and get going. The first person I met was Scott Gendron. He was ashen faced and unbelieving, and we talked about the whole thing.

He had been told to get out, but he had decided that they didn't need to. Then they were asked again at 6:00, and he thought better. He gave me a brief history of what had happened there, and that some of his cars were on top of Rock Wilson's and the water had gotten under the slab in the basement of his house and forced it straight up in the air. His daughter's bedroom and his living room were down there, and he showed me all of that. He suggested how I might actually get to the center of the town. He said that I would get no further south, and he said I wouldn't get east of his house. He suggested that I go down a little further then go up over the bank and try to get to Fred Roentsch's mansion in Langdon. So I did, and was headed in that direction when I came to some water I couldn't quite get over. A man and a boy were walking towards me with… I think it was a piece of a garage door. A folding garage door with four panels, and they had one panel. They got close enough to holler to, and I said, "Is that going to be a bridge?" And they said, "Well, yeah!" and I said, "Great!", so they threw it across, and I caught the end of it and I was the first to cross over the garage door bridge. I got to about where Warren Brook crossing is at the Crumps, and I had to do something else, so I went up over the hill. It was quite steep there, and I had to climb up on hands and knees.

Then down the hill again, jumped the water again, and came out into a backyard that was on Griffin Hill Road. I don't know whose house it was, but I came out and got to Gary Gendron's house where a man was standing, talking on a cell phone. I hollered, I felt like I was in a disaster movie, "Does that phone work?" He said, "Yeah, it does." And I met Brian Greene. He was there with Gary Gendron's wife, who was on the garage floor surrounded by rifles. Apparently, they belonged to Scott Gendron, who had ferried them up by ATV to higher ground. She was busy wiping them off, drying them out, and so forth. I called my sister in Hinsdale to let her know that my mother and I were all right. Brian asked if he could take Gary's old truck sitting in the driveway to get me to Fred Roentsch. Gary's wife said that that would be all right, so we got in that and drove up to Dan Metcalf, and then down in what is now a class six road to Dave French's, down that way to Fred Roentsch's, and the going was pretty good that way. We continued on and went up to the McDermott Bridge. Then up Winch Hill to Langdon, then down Eggerton Hill to Pleasant Street. I was driven all the way to the other side of the bridge, to the village.

Interviewer: How long did this journey take?
Matt Saxton: Three and a half hours for what would normally take ten minutes.

At this time we were seeing the water build, the debris starting to block the [Drewsville] bridge. I remember our Langdon police chief [Ray L'Abbe] was down in their driveway, pleading with them to get in their car and drive out. They were running out of time. They probably [had] three to four minutes before there was no access to the bridge.

I had climbed up on the bank a little bit and remember hearing over our fire radios reports of where this wall of water was, and the last report I'd heard was that it was behind the gun shop, and it was about that time that there was an indescribable sound. You know, I just don't know what it sounds like to describe. It was a combination of the roar of the water, everything that it had gathered, pulling trees, and just a real indescribable noise of it coming… And then I believe that it was Rock Wilson's outside

Buildings carried by the Cold River over the Drewsville Bridge and into the gorge on right. *Photographs by Ray L'Abbe*

furnace that came down through; it was upright in the water with smoke still coming up out of the chimney stack. I just had to kind of chuckle to myself to think of that coming down through. And then all of a sudden I looked and I said, 'Here comes Jeannette's trailer.' It was washed off its foundation. There were some trees there down by where the pull-off used to be, and the water just kind of washed it down through those trees. She had a front porch on it; it ripped that off. The trailer hit the rails on the bridge. The water is up over now with the debris and stuff, and just kind of kicked it sideways; it held there for like thirty seconds. The trailer just spun around over where you access the bridge from Cheshire turnpike Langdon side, kicked it down, down over into the gorge, and you could hear it smashing apart.

Shelley Barnes

Damage to the Drewsville Bridge. *Photograph by Steve Fortier*

In only twenty-four minutes, the water unleashed by the collapse of Cooper Hill Road had traveled four miles down the narrow river valley on which most of Alstead Village lies. It would continue on down river from Alstead Village for miles, through the Drewsville Gorge and beyond, flooding fields and destroying the landmark North Walpole Stone Bridge, before at last disgorging into the Connecticut River. The damage left in its wake was shocking, unprecedented in the town's 242-year history. Nearly fifty homes and businesses were damaged or destroyed by the rising water and flood wave. In the confusion dozens of people were reported missing, many of them feared dead.

Despite the fact that one of the few intact roads to Alstead Village was blocked by a fallen tree, people from outlying parts of the town quickly began to come down from the hills.

The Cold River flood collapsed this 1908-09 stone arch bridge in North Walpole. *Photograph by Nicholas Brown*

"I think a lot of people hadn't realized how severe the damage was," said Anton Elbers, who had witnessed the flood surge's passage through the heart of the community. "There's just that curiosity of a big event, and people were a little bit in shock. It had that similar feeling to some of the large gatherings—you know, the festival in Alstead, or something—where people are greeting each other on the street and running into people that they may not have seen for a while. There was an element of amazement and shock that it happened and that it could happen there."

Told by a family friend of the devastation of the town below, eight-year-old Colleen Heidorn could only express disbelief. Indeed, many in the area were unable or unwilling to accept that what had just happened was real, but as the light brightened under an overcast sky, the scope of the disaster could not be denied.

"I felt shock," Derek Sherburne remembered, having made his way with his brother Jesse into the center of town from their home inside the old Vilas mansion. "You know, I was just…"

"Helpless," his brother continued. "Helpless. He didn't know what to do. There was so much stuff to do. I mean you've got people walking up and down the road that you've known all of your life, and they're shocked. Their houses are gone. You don't know what to say to them, what to do."

Alstead man contemplates the complete loss of homes on Forest Road near the Sweeney home (in background). *Photograph by Wayne and Patty Hatch*

> *The horrible, terrible flood of 2005 almost washed Alstead off the map.*
>
> *~ Paige O'Dette (age 12)*

As the morning turned into afternoon, townspeople and emergency officials began to make their way up and down the river from the center of town. Downstream, the devastation was terrible. Homes and buildings in the path of the raging torrent had been erased, hillsides had vanished, mountains of debris marred farmland, and the distant Drewsville Bridge barely hung onto its foundation. All who ventured near the wide swath of destruction echoed the sentiments of Delvina Kearney, the owner of the general store: "To know that such devastation could happen. It's not supposed to happen here. Bangladesh or somewhere, but not in our backyard."

Upriver, the damage was more severe. Houses that had dotted the landscape for generations stood empty, their sides and foundations swept away. Kmiec's Garage, a local landmark, had been so utterly destroyed that not even the land on which it had stood was recognizable. The road up to the maw that had once been Cooper Hill Road and its culvert had also received the brunt of the surge. The force of the flood wave had torn away innumerable sections, stranding those who still lived between Lake Warren and Alstead Village. "I didn't think it was going to be that bad," remembered fifth-grader Angela Hilow, whose own home was lost to the river. "I didn't think that the whole road was going to be missing, a whole chunk of it… I thought that the land was still going to be there, but when you got there you couldn't see anything; the trees were down and everything."

Floodwaters at Alstead Village Bridge. *Photographer unknown*

Near Warren Brook

Stella Winham and her daughter Maggie Gacek spent Saturday night in the Winham house on Warren Brook's bank. Maggie Gacek shares her story about Sunday morning.

I heard the phone and jumped out of bed, came out in the middle room, and she said it was [Uncle] Pard, and he said we gotta get out. And we both ran down stairs. There's two stairways in the house, one right in the middle, and one going out the front. We ran down the one into the dining room, and the water was up over the window, and I screamed at her to get back up stairs. We were running back upstairs, and I'm not sure if we were on the foundation then or not. I have no concept of moving, strange as it sounds. The noise was deafening, just deafening, the roar. Huge, huge roar. And the kitchen door was blowing out right in front of me. Something took over, something took over. Get to higher ground! That voice, the wonderful voice, I'm so glad it showed up. Get upstairs now! That's all I could think of. Mom and me would have… My bedroom was gone at the top of the stairs. I had just got out of it, and it was gone. […]

We moved into the middle of the room, and my mother has a cat, and she said get Suzie, and I looked and it's coming up the stairs. I hope she's up here, because I knew I wasn't going back down. And we had these brief moments of do we go out the window, or do we go out the door? I'm so glad I didn't act on that one. And then the whole concept of we weren't even where we were.

The house was gone. My bedroom was gone, so we must have moved. It sounds so stupid, but it was so incomprehensible that… And I thought the rest of the house was going to fold up like a house of cards, and we were still in it. The water's gotta go… The reality of what happened, and seeing all this stuff going by. It looked like something out of the movies, where you see the people, and the houses going by, and this horrendous wave going by. We saw it, but the mind said that's too awful to see. To realize that we were not on the foundation either, and realize maybe that house was going down the river too.

There were like three rooms to the house, and we always looked like Little House on the Prairie, you had all these beds lined up. We were in the middle, and I got her housecoat on her, she had clothes upstairs. My clothes were in the bedroom, which was no longer there. I'm gonna leave naked, I knew it. This is not the way I'm going! Got some boots on her, and she just kept saying that we're not going to die. We're not going to die. And I went on automatic… I don't know. That's the only thing I asked God for. Let me do whatever I'm supposed to do right now. The conscious thought of dying was not conscious. It was there in the back of my mind, but… I just wanted to make sure my mother was all right. I prayed for the water to go down. I knew we would get out then. I didn't realize that we weren't where we were. But the cat was upstairs, the cat was under the bed.

Paul Besaw's son and grandson were walking up and down the road yelling to see if anybody was anywhere, and I called to them and they came over. They came up the front stairs, which were half there, and helped us out. And then we had to get out of there. We went up to his house; he didn't have any power or any water. Very little water. But he was on much higher ground. The power lines were down. This is so stupid, I'm like terrified, the power lines were down everywhere. I'm like don't get near them, but the power was dead! Later, they said the power lines are down, they're dead, but they were everywhere. We had to get over them, and it was like 'Oh my god, we're going to get electrocuted!'"

"It looked like a war zone to me," said Erwin Ward, life-long resident and Air Force veteran. "It made me think I was back in Germany, in a war zone."

Looking east on the remains of Forest Road.
Photograph by Dale Dustin

Looking west on the remains of Forest Road. Sweeney house in background.
Photograph by Eleanor Elbers

Car lodged in tree on site of Jeannette Clark's former home.
Photograph by Heather Gendron

Arial view of Warren Brook and Forest Road 0.6 miles downstream from Cooper Hill Road. Remains of Cooper Hill Road culvert rests infront of Larsen home. Sheldon and Nichols homes in upper right.
Photograph by Heather Gendron

Kmiec's Garage

"Kmiec's has always been there since I've been in town," Almut Yakovleff remembers. "My car has always gone there. They're wonderful people and they've helped me a lot. It's almost like, they're part of this town—I mean it's not an historical marker, but—" she trailed off, perhaps assuming that everyone in Alstead knew what she meant. Most likely they did.

Kmiec's garage had been around since 1943 when it was built on the opposite side of the road. Ten years later, the state wanted to widen the road, and Kmiec's pumps were in the way, so it was rebuilt on the river-side of the road, in the location it still held in early October of 2005. Stanley Kmiec, Senior, was the original owner, and he worked in the garage with his brother John. He would later pass the business to his son Stanley "Sonny" Kmiec, who would later sell it to John Rowan, a cousin by marriage. For most residents, Kmiec's Garage was something that had always been a landmark in the town, and with its solid cinderblock structure, it seemed like it always would.

Kmiec's Garage, built in 1943, picture taken 10 years later. *Photograph courtesy of Brad and Kitty Kmiec.*

Kmiec's Garage in August 2005. *Photograph courtesy of Town of Alstead*

Underground fuel tanks at the site of Kmiec's Garage which was completely destroyed by the flood. *Photograph by Joe Szuch*

> *There was mud everywhere you go.*
>
> ~ Kevin Plummer (age 12)

Despite the best efforts of Police Chief Christopher Lyons and many other emergency workers to evacuate all of the houses in the river's path, many long-time residents had refused to leave, and now that the waters had receded, locating and rescuing them took top priority. When Selectman Matt Saxton finally managed to arrive at the makeshift disaster relief headquarters in the fire station, he jumped at the chance to take part in the effort. Along with Jack Michnovez, he left to find Stella Winham, whose house was right in the middle of the devastation, largely cut off by washed-out roads and areas where the river was still flooded. Taking a town truck through a winding network of back roads, the two finally found a way into the heart of the disaster.

Stella Winham's former bedroom.
Photograph by Linda Putnam

Stella Winham's house after the flood.
Photograph by David and Julie Hogan

We went to the bottom of Cobb Hill and left the truck there. We had a flashlight and a rope, and Jack is a former police chief from a small town in western Massachusetts, so he had some idea of what to do. I talked to him about that, and said, 'Jack, am I prepared for this? What if I see a hand or an arm stick out of a bunch of debris, you know?' We decided not to think about it and just kept going, and he gave me brief instructions. He told me you wanted to look beside, under, over, through, and keep moving. By that time, someone had already been through that valley because there were already messages spray-painted on the houses: Zero people at 10:00 a.m. We didn't go in those because they'd obviously already been checked, but we were looking in the debris for what we might find. It was just amazing, in that pile of trees there was part of a sofa and a muffin tin, part of a coffee maker, blanket, and a bathtub. Anything and everything was scattered everywhere.

We got to Stella Winham's house, and the front of it was torn off, but otherwise, it was sort of whole. Jack was poking around, and I said I would check the house. The downstairs of the house was wrecked, but I got upstairs to what was Stella's bedroom. It was tilted by a foot and a half or so, but otherwise whole. The covers were turned down as they would be if someone was getting out of bed on an average morning. Her glasses were on the stand. They looked undisturbed, but her glasses weren't with

Painted messages on buildings made during searches for missing persons. Home of Ray and Mary Moore is shown here. *Photograph by Dale Guinn*

After the water went down, my family and my neighbors walked through the hole downtown.

~Jacadi Simard (age 11)

> *The flood took a lot of things; a lot of them can't be replaced.*
>
> ~Sabrina Sodders (age 11)

her, wherever she was. I thought, well, it looks peaceful enough, but if she left, she would have taken her glasses. So I looked all around and I couldn't find anything, but the closet door was closed. I thought at this point, would someone run into a closet? I couldn't get the closet door open because the house was so wrecked, but I decided I wasn't going to leave without that closet door. I yanked on it enough, and I guess the adrenaline was pumping, because I broke the door in half. The closet was full of other stuff. No Stella.

We left and we kept going, and by this time Peter Rhoades and his son Randy had shown up. They were sort of poking around in the same search and rescue efforts we were. They had got ahead of us and were maybe a hundred yards ahead, and suddenly Peter is running at us, screaming, 'I've found her!' And I thought, 'Oh, dear god.' We weren't really watching them, and as he got closer, he said 'She's at Besaw's!' So they hadn't found her in the rubble. They had found her at Besaw's.

So we ran up to Besaw's, and Jack was behind me, and Stella's daughter opened the door, and I look past her, and Stella was lying on the day bed. I brushed by Margaret and rushed over to Stella and took her up in my arms, and said, 'You don't know how happy I am to find you in this condition!' and she said to me, 'All the things I was going to sell you are gone.' I said, 'For crying out loud, Stella, it's just stuff. Don't worry about stuff. My god, you're alive! This is wonderful!' It was just that I would have never expected her to say that. Our minds were just swimming at a time like that.

Matt Saxton

As Matt Saxton made his way back to town to report that Stella Winham was safe and to assist in the coordination of fledgling relief efforts, he passed many stupefied townspeople, making their way over piles of debris and around vast holes in the road. Some had come simply to see what had really occurred. Others came to determine what had become of their homes. The Perry's house had been one of the closest to the blown culvert. Sharon Perry remembered what she found:

There was nothing there. Nothing. All that day and the next day, all I was thinking is that there was no sign. All of our lives, we've been married for thirty-four years, and everything that we'd ever worked for had been put into that. Everything we ever owned. Everything. And it's like it hadn't ever even existed. And I didn't know how to take that. If you had pinched me, I don't even think if I would have felt it. It's like I wasn't ever there. There was nothing on this Earth to even show that I had even existed.

Site of the former Perry home on Forest Road just below Cooper Hill Road. The only remnant of the home is the well pipe. *Photograph by Robert Larsen*

> *The gas, oil and propane made the water so you couldn't drink or use it.*
>
> ~Zachary Garrow (age 12)

Though the destruction was somewhat less severe above the breach where the culvert had been, the long night of rushing waters had left homes in ruins and damaged roadways beyond recognition. When Eleanor Elbers made her way down to Chase's Mill, located at the intersection between Lake Warren and the valley below, she stared at the landscape in amazement.

> The [Prentice Hill Road] bridge was washed out. There was this huge river where there used to be a road that used to go up to the Chase's house. You couldn't tell at that point. You couldn't tell if the dam had broken…it was like an earthquake had hit. There wasn't like a little gully out of it, which I saw in other areas; it was like a completely destroyed road. There was nothing there. There were broken lumps and then deep, deep crevasses, like seven feet deep along the sides. It was like cliffs. It was something we have never seen.

Back in the village, the list of people reported missing mounted. As news of what had occurred in Alstead spread, more and more people began to call whomever they could for information, chief among them Delvina Kearney, who kept the village store open throughout the day.

Viewing the damage. *Photograph by Steve Hooper, courtesy of* The Keene Sentinel, *October 16, 2005*

Residents console one another. *Photograph by Kathy Torrey*

Townspeople examine flood damages. *Photograph by Stacy Eaton*

Opposite page:

Chase's Mill, East Alsread, on Sunday morning. *Photograph by Betsy Anderson*

> *The water looked like water you could go white-water rafting on.*
>
> *~ Mary Locke (age 12)*

The phone rang here all the time. This was kind of the base. There was no police station; it was gone, wiped out. Who do you call? I was getting phone calls all day long: 'How are you?' 'What's going on?' 'Have you seen this person?' 'Can I talk to that person?' So our phones worked the whole time. [It's] unbelievable how our phones worked all day.

My most horrifying moment was when I found out that Bill Seale's wife…She had called me five times on Sunday. 'Has anybody seen Bill Seale?' I didn't know who Bill Seale was, not until afterwards realizing he was the gentleman I had bought my marigolds from this summer. He had the honor system: you put the money in the pot and take the flowers. Being new this year, I didn't know a lot of the people; I do now. The names, the familiarity, it was really hard, I was really frustrated, just not knowing people and just wanting to help, but I couldn't help.

Delvina Kearney

That afternoon was perhaps the darkest time in Alstead's history. Yet, for all of the sorrow, the confusion, the loss, the people of the town began to pull together. Randy Kmiec, whose grandparents had owned the destroyed garage, watched as people came to terms with the tragedy. "First everybody stood there with their mouths open like, 'What happened?' and then everybody just wanted to start helping."

With shovels, with personal construction and farming equipment, with bare hands, people, some of whom had never met one another before, began to help sift through the rubble for cherished belongings. Others assembled in the meeting hall behind the fire station, looking for some way to help their now homeless neighbors and friends. And with the next dawn, the outpouring of support and relief would only grow stronger.

Even after a long day of searching, the scale of the disaster was hard for many to comprehend and all the more so for the town's leaders. Police Chief Christopher Lyons, who had managed to secure a helicopter to assist in the recovery effort, was disheartened by just how changed the landscape had become. "There was no area that was safe to land a helicopter. There was just too much debris. It looked like a combination of a flood and an earthquake… It looked like a war zone."

6 Griffin Hill Road

Bill Seale had lived in Alstead for thirty-nine of his sixty-four years and was perhaps the epitome of the New England farmer with his impeccable work ethic and curt disposition. "Bill had a kind of gruff way about him," said his wife Linda Anderson, "but he really meant well."

Linda and Bill had been married one rainy day more than fifteen years earlier. When Linda met him, Bill was selling woodstoves, but since then, Bill's passion for farming had come to the forefront of their lives.

"He probably grew about ten acres or so of vegetable gardens, and he did maple sugaring. We had…I would say four or five greenhouses at our house. He would always…have a lot of plants in the greenhouse. He would use flowers to start the market off with, and he'd also start vegetable plants because people would buy the plants plus he would use them to plant in the ground. He went to the Keene Farmers' Market; he was their largest vendor there. That was his livelihood, our livelihood. So he took the flowers in the springtime and early plants—asparagus and early things that came up—and maple syrup, of course; he made maple syrup, and we shipped it all over the world.

And in the summer I baked for the farmers market and made breads and muffins and jams and jellies…We also had a stand…across from the garden, and people would come by. He used the honor system, which people don't really use now.

…Bill, that was his life, and he just worked hard at doing the farming."

So Bill was a familiar figure in the area, providing residents with vegetables and flowers, berries and syrup that was boiled down in his makeshift sugarhouse: the garage. Their home was always filled with flowers; it became a joke between the couple: "He would bring flowers home all the time, and I said, 'This is beginning to look like a funeral home!'"

Bill and Linda knew the power of water. Less than three months ago hurricane Katrina had ripped through the city of New Orleans, breaching the levees and unleashing the surrounding waters on the city's inhabitants. "My son Chris lived there," said Linda. "Well, Katrina came and my son Chris became homeless…and I thought that was the worst thing that could happen."

When I first saw all the damage that was done, I felt like a sucker punch in the stomach.

~ Sarah DeValk -age 11.

Working all the rest of the day to coordinate rescue efforts from the fire station, Matt Saxton met one of the first external aid groups to make its way into the village center.

> Then the young Lieutenant arrived with the National Guard. He presented himself, and I said, "Awfully glad to see you, young man. What have you brought with you?'"
> He said, "What?'
> "Well, how many?"
> "We are eight."
> "What have you brought with you?"
> He said, "We've got a backhoe and a dump truck."
> And I said, "Well, young man, I am very glad to see you here. It's dark right now, but in the morning you will understand why you are so woefully under-equipped."

As night fell over the ravaged valley, its people anxiously awaited the next morning and the days and weeks that would follow. Bill Seale, along with Tim and Sally Canfield, and Spencer Petty were still missing. Basic utilities like electricity and telephone service were knocked out all over the town. Cell phone service was mostly nonexistent. The sheer amount of damage that homes and the land itself had received made recovery and restoration seem impossible. More than that, the threat posed by the overtaxed Warren Dam and warnings of another rainstorm deepened their sense of discouragement. Sunday was just a day of not knowing. If that was the worst of it, what else was going to happen? Was Lake Warren going to let go?

Walking west on Forest Road. *Photograph by Bob Brown*

Overcoming Chaos

> *There was mud everywhere you go. There were also boulders rolling all over the place.*
>
> *~ Kevin Plummer (age 12)*

Overleaf:
A resident explores the new terrain.
Photograph by Nicholas Brown

Neighbor Helping Neighbor

"The actual event itself happened so fast that no one had time to get a mood," Alstead resident Meredith Howard remembered when asked what the town's initial response to the disaster had been. "Then afterwards, I thought that everybody was remarkable. They came together, and nobody was putting any blame on things, we just got it together and did it. What had to be done. The National Guard and the State Police and whoever else was in here; they were always polite to us. They were wonderful. They didn't try to take over our lives very much."

Her sentiments were shared by almost everyone who still remained in the village. For all of the fear, loss, and confusion that the flood had sown in its wake, the resilience of the little town was remarkable. As Monday dawned over the Cold River valley, work that had been set in motion the previous day began again in earnest. The National Guard had already arrived, and many other emergency units and relief organizations would soon follow: the New Hampshire State Police, the Red Cross, the Federal Emergency Management Agency (FEMA), and the Salvation Army, all eager to assist beleaguered local officials and residents. As Matt Saxton remembered, the sudden influx of aid was somewhat overwhelming:

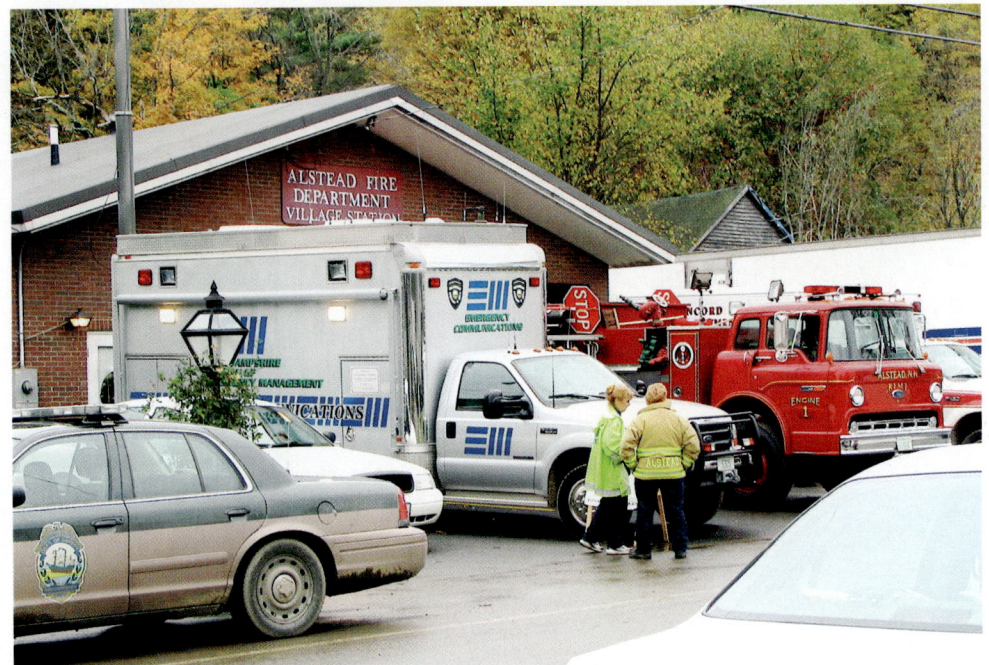

The Fire Station served as the command center for emergency operations.
Photograph by Mike Heidorn

I walked into the command center, and I said, 'Who is in charge?' because I certainly couldn't tell. I mean, there were uniforms all over the place. The ranking of who reports to whom wasn't clear, it had never been written down—at least that I saw. So, as a selectman, I felt sort of superfluous because everything had been taken over. I walked around and made myself available.

The newly designated command center, focal point of all emergency operations for weeks to come, was located in the back room of the fire station, a place normally used for town meetings and Friendly Meals. "It had some funny name, Incident Command Center or something," Selectman Joel McCarty remembered. "That worked out okay because every bit of information that flowed in and out of town went through that room." The place originally intended to coordinate disaster relief, should the need arise, was now coated inside and out by layers of mud and debris. Boarded up by Chief Lyons to prevent unauthorized access the previous day, the police station had been ruined, even though the second floor of the building was intact. "Every wire and radiator and square inch of sheet rock downstairs was destroyed. Every paper, business machine, radio, and telephone was trashed," McCarty reported grimly.

National Guard personnel move up Acworth Road toward Vilas Pool. *Photograph by Steve Fortier*

The land was gone also. How could they rebuild without land?

~Jeremy Barnett (age 12)

One of the immediate problems raised by the destroyed police station was that all emergency calls had to be redirected to the police department in the nearby city of Keene. Keene had to deal with its own flooding caused by the storm and could not handle the extra burden. To respond to local calls, police secretary Michelle Koson, who had barely escaped when the flood wave hit the police station, set up a makeshift dispatch center on the upper floor of the town office building, only a few feet above what remained of the police station. Delvina Kearney offered the upper floor of the Village Market as a more stable location, and a mobile command center was also briefly considered. Then the neighboring town of Langdon offered the use of the empty Baker building, which was spacious and better suited to the long job that lay ahead.

After the first few days, order at last began to reestablish itself. "Joel McCarty was the designated emergency management director," said Matt Saxton. "He conceded immediately to Kim Kercewich, Fire Chief. By Monday and Tuesday the town hall was crowded with uniforms of all description. There was the State Police; there was Fish & Game; there was Search & Rescue; there was the Sheriff's Department." McCarty elaborated:

Tyler Gendron and Lyle Doolittle look at the remains of the Cooper Hill Road culvert. *Photograph by Heather Gendron*

The people playing the lead role, I think, would be the New Hampshire Bureau of Emergency Management, my principal ally in the endless paper chase dealing with the federal government. Those guys had a pretty good system in place for emergency communications, and they parked a big truck out in front of the fire station. It wasn't long afterward that other state agencies started showing up with police patrols to secure the borders of town and make themselves visible so that we didn't have any trouble with the looting that was reported—that was reported to us, anyway. We got a lot of help from fire department personnel, from that sort of broad brotherhood of men and women and rescue people who didn't actually have any fires to put out and hardly anybody to rescue, but it was nice to have them here, and they were certainly willing to fill in. They did a lot of search and rescue work under the supervision of some teams from the Department for Resources and Economic Development and the fish and game guys. The Cheshire County Sheriff Department had a big presence here; they got some help from the Sullivan County Sheriff Department. It wasn't very long before the governor sent the National Guard over, and they were here for a couple of weeks. State police were here, of course, state police from Vermont and New Hampshire and Massachusetts, I think. The Red Cross set up some cooking stuff right away. We already had kind of a kitchen in the town hall, so we were in pretty good shape in terms of feeding people.

Despite some initial uncertainty, the influx of assistance was met with open arms and had little difficulty finding places to take root. "We opened our doors and became the second Red Cross site," said the Reverend Jan Howe of the Third Congregational Church of Alstead. "We also acted as a Salvation Army center and shelter; we also provided Friendly Meals." Pallets of food and essential supplies from uncounted charity groups and corporations like BJ's and Wal-Mart were stored in local businesses and greenhouses. Families opened their doors to those who had been left homeless.

Unloading supplies from the Churches of Christ disaster relief truck at BE Supply on Route 12A. *Photograph by Minnie Haskins*

With support structures in place, emergency personnel and state workers were eager to begin clean-up, to restore basic utilities like phone service and electricity, and to search for those who were still listed among the missing.

Soon the village was alive with focused activity. The speed at which the work began even created some misconceptions in the state and national media, which were only beginning to find their way to this out-of-the-way town.

The Third Congregational Church on River Street served as a Salvation Army center and shelter. *Photograph by David Moody*

The white rock with the memorial plaque in it was picked up by the AP wire service. The picture shows the white rock that was "washed by the floodwaters and came to rest in front of the library." I laughed every time I saw that, because, at some point Sunday afternoon, I realized that we were going to have to clean this mess up. I had heard on the radio about how they had a central debris field, down in New Orleans, a place where they took stuff, where it could be sorted and recycled properly. So I decided that Millot Green would be the place to do that. Somebody with a backhoe was standing beside me. I said, "Pick up that white rock," which was about fifteen feet from where it had started in the Millot. I said, "Put it over in front of the library."

Matt Saxton

The placement of that white rock is no longer evidence of the ferocity of nature. It is a testament to the resilience of a town and its people.

Alstead Memorial Rock rests in front of the Shedd Porter Library.
Photograph by Michael Moore, courtesy of The Keene Sentinel, *October 12, 2005.*

"A lot of times on the news you'll hear New Hampshire is the stingiest state in the nation," commented David Crosby. "Well, it may be by their accounts, but I beg to differ. The amount of help that has come into this town, and the other towns too, from private donations and everything is unbelievable."

After the floodwaters of Sunday morning had passed through, there were dozens of families who had been left without homes or possessions. They gathered at the fire station, at local churches, at the homes of friends. Most were lost, confused, and hopeless. It was a state that few of their neighbors could bear to see, and so they pledged their homes, time, money, and labor to ensure that the flood victims would pull through.

To complement the Red Cross and Salvation Army units, the members of the Third Congregational Church offered their building and time for whatever services were needed. "Our doors were open for more than a month, and we were the FEMA base for operation. We had an Always-Here help line. We also set up an account for incoming relief fund money called the Alstead Flood Relief Fund."

Emergency-service organizations begin work in Alstead. *Photographer unknown*

Students at the nearby Fall Mountain Regional High School pitched in as well. Karri Makinen raised money for the flood victims by collecting money outside Shaw's supermarket in Walpole with a friend during the week they were out of school. They raised over two thousand dollars. "We were out of school and felt we had to do something to help… I was really surprised how generous people were… A lot of people who were donors were victims themselves, just wanting to help people in greater need."

Among the most generous and active contributors to the relief effort was a group made up of five local women, Martha Cooper, Pam Allen, Mary Ann Melquist, Fran Thibault, and Tammy Hutchinson, which was officially named The Alstead Flood Relief Volunteers, but more widely and fondly known as the "Flood Babes."

> The Flood Babes have come together with very little help from the selectmen and managed to organize and raise and distribute more money in private aid than FEMA has delivered to private households in this town, so it's really quite an extraordinary group and they will continue to work for us at least another year. They really came out of nowhere and simply

The Federal Emergency Management Agency (FEMA) set up shop in the back of the Third Congregational Church. Reflected in mirror, left to right, church Trustees Hans Waldman and Robert Young spoke with FEMA staffers Sunday afternoon, November 6, about available flood aid. *Photograph by Paul Garcia, courtesy of The Keene Sentinel, November 7, 2005*

> *People are helping each other and fixing things up.*
>
> ~Alexis Burns (age 11)

pushed their way to the front of the room at one meeting and said, 'You know what, we don't actually know how we can help but we're going to be in your office tomorrow morning at 8:00 and you'd better find something for us to do.' So I said 'Cool.' And that's worked out extremely well.

Joel McCarty

The first two months were absolute chaos. We didn't eat a hot meal. We ate candy off the table here. After January, we at least knew the turf. People were mostly settled in. When the cold weather came, everybody was hunkered down. Then it became more problematic, working with different programs. We applied for everything we could—it was an enormous amount of work. We became experts overnight because we had to. It went from one thing to another. I can remember a month into it, I walked past Joel and he said, "If you can stay with this until February (it was November), I'll name the Town Barn for you!" [Mary Ann laughs] You just had no idea what you were getting into. I think one of the reasons we stay is because we're a team and a damn good one. People still need us. I appreciate a good team.

Mary Ann Melquist

The Alstead Historical Society Museum on High Street served as a warehouse for donated furniture and household items. *Photographs by Nicholas Brown*

"We've all benefited by working together," added Martha Cooper concerning the group's role as a donation center. "People were so generous. We were a conduit. Hundreds of thousands of dollars we could give out. And flood families were so generous with their time and their privacy being invaded. It kept the money coming—the media stories kept everything alive."

Businesses, local and national alike, were also very generous in donations of bottled water, food, generators, and other much needed supplies. Wal-Mart alone delivered uncounted boxes of cots, blankets, socks, cleaning supplies, and anything else that might be wanted. A motel donated dozens of beds, mattresses, bureaus, lamps, and other furniture. Even the most unlikely things found their way into donation centers. "A cardboard box of fennel," Matt Saxton remembered. "I tried to find things to laugh about."

And the donations weren't all material, either. Some, like the Southern Baptist Disaster Relief, provided emotional support.

> "The Friday before they left," remembered Paul Garatoni, "they stopped by, and they came in and we talked. One gentleman, the tall guy from Derry, says, 'Do you mind if we give you a blessing?'
> I said, "Mind? Thank you!"
> He says, "Do you mind if we sing it?"
> "Can you sing good?"
> "Well, you tell me."
> And they sang us the sweetest little blessing on us and our house and our town and everybody, and all you've gotta say is thank you. Be you a religious man or not, if you can't appreciate somebody praying to their spiritual leader, you say thanks. I don't care if he's a Muslim, a Christian, a Jew, or an agnostic atheist, a Druid! If you're praying for me, man, I just say thanks.

One of the greatest and most needed services provided with the help of some of the townspeople was cooking. In addition to dozens of displaced residents, hundreds of emergency personnel, some of whom were working 100-hour weeks, needed to be fed, and fed they were. From two locations on either side of the river, Red Cross, Salvation Army workers, and Friendly Meals volunteers labored over stoves and ovens morning, noon, and night. "In that whole two weeks, they cooked bacon every morning," recalled Matt Saxton. "I don't know how much, it must have been pounds and pounds and pounds of bacon every morning. Because all these people were here, and they had to eat."

> *My mom's giving all the food at our house to the people at the fire station.*
>
> *~Alex Kercewich (age 5)*

When the rivers stopped rushing, everybody got right to work.

~Josh Sullivan (age 12)

"We'd stay at the hall until 5 P.M.," said Mary Lou Huffling, coordinator as well as one of the volunteers who cooked for Friendly Meals at the local Masonic Hall. "I figured out not long ago, since the flood, over thirty thousand volunteer hours have been given to the Food Shelf and to Friendly Meals. Our youngest volunteer is 5 and our oldest ones are in their 80's. People who had suffered directly from the flood often offered and did help at the Food Shelf and at meals."

"I don't think I ever ate so well in my life," said Police Chief Lyons, recalling a pineapple upside-down cake that was served one evening. "I remember the meals that the Salvation Army would prepare…I don't want to say it was good times, but it was a nice feeling to sit down, work with these people and share a meal. It was something that you just may never experience again."

> I wanted to know what was happening and how widespread this is… Is this just Alstead? Is it Alstead, Marlow, and Keene? I had heard that Keene was bad, [but] we don't have any TV.
>
> *Eleanor Elbers*

Although Alstead Village was the epicenter of the disaster, the torrential rains and flood damage of October 8th and 9th had not been isolated to a single river valley. All throughout Cheshire, Sullivan, and Hillsboro counties, basements were flooded and roads washed away.

Alstead women prepare a meal for emergency workers at The Masonic Hall in Langdon.
Photograph by Steve Fortier

Forty percent of the City of Keene was underwater, and the neighboring communities of Walpole, Acworth, Langdon, and Unity all suffered extensive damage. Several bridges across the Connecticut River's tributaries had been disabled or completely washed away. Utilities throughout the region were disrupted, and some areas lacked power and phone service for many days afterwards. All told, eleven people statewide died from accidents stemming from the storm.

Even so, the outpouring of assistance and support from nearby towns was astonishing. Although many communities would have been wholly justified in keeping their emergency personnel and equipment to clean up their own damage, police, firefighters, ambulance services, and road workers from all over New Hampshire supplemented the ranks of state, federal and private organizations in Alstead. "I think that was another thing that struck me," Dale Dustin stated that "just within a couple days of the flood, seeing rescue equipment, seeing fire equipment, from Nashua, from Plymouth… it struck me that we're not in this alone."

Taylor Welding's eagle keeps an eye on emergency services workers. *Photograph by Paul Garcia*

Three firemen from around the state of New Hampshire surveyed the damage to Alstead Village.
Photograph by Mike Wright.

Shelley Barnes, herself a Langdon Fire and Rescue captain, reflected:

> A lot of neighbors, not necessarily next door but surrounding towns, reached out to offer assistance. It's just nice, especially just prior to this event here they had the terrible hurricanes going through Louisiana and Mississippi. It's just eye-opening to us how a tragic event can bring people together, if they'll allow it.

Governor John Lynch himself traveled to Alstead and the surrounding area five times in the days after the disaster, personally thanking those who were aiding in the relief and reviewing early clean-up plans. "It's unbelievable, the devastation and destruction. We've never seen anything like it," he told the CNN national news network.[23] He did express hope for the future, however. "I can tell you, here in New Hampshire, we're all working together. There's excellent communication: excellent communication among the department heads, excellent communication between the state departments and civic leaders, between state and private companies, between myself and the congressional delegation."

Left to right: N.H. State Senator Bob Odell, Governor John Lynch, and Alstead Police Chief Christopher Lyons view flood damage on Millot Green in Alstead. *Photograph by Paul Garcia, courtesy of* The River Record

News crews came from across New England and broadcast what was happening to the rest of the country.

~Daniel Gendron (age 11)

Unfortunately, not everyone who made their way into Alstead was there to help. Delvina Kearney remembered:

> People were coming in and you heard about people looting stuff. You really just wanted to believe that wasn't happening. A lot of it was out-of-town people. It was not the local people. These people were coming in and just grabbing what they could, and it didn't belong to them. I mean, how could you do that? If you wanted to take it and bring it somewhere, that's fine, but a lot of people were just loading up their cars and leaving with it…I never saw that, but I heard about it.
>
> Bobbie Wilson, for one. A lady was standing on her porch and Bobbie went up and said, "What are you doing here?"
>
> "Well, I'm curious."
>
> And Bobbie said, "This is my home. Get out."
>
> I think a lot of people felt violated that people were coming in. They had lost so much, and people came because they want to get a feel or a sense of what's happening. I don't think a lot of people realized that they were violating [other] people's privacy. And that's when the first sign came up: GAWKERS GO AWAY!

Governor Lynch thanks Delvina Kearney in the Alstead Village Market. *Photograph by Michael Moore, courtesy of The Keene Sentinel, October 13, 2005*

Though impressive in its blunt simplicity, that large, makeshift warning did not daunt the crowds of news media who braved rain and damaged roads to get videotapes of the destruction and those who had survived it. "The press wants me to make a sensational statement…" sighed Tom Hancock, one of many who were approached by reporters in search of perspective on the tragedy.

Some residents didn't mind the increased attention. Approached by a news team from WMUR, the regional TV network, Paul Garatoni was glad to point out that his home was nearly broken in half. "You could see paint stretching, honest to god. They took some pictures, and I was on Channel Nine with it, and I took them through. I said, "Make sure you get a picture of the paint that held my house together."

WMUR-TV truck from Manchester, New Hampshire, arrives in Alstead. *Photograph by David Collins*

> *After the flood, the beautiful town of Alstead looked like a dump.*
>
> ~Tyler Gendron (age 11)

When they became too invasive, however, the media did pose a problem, both to the still-recovering residents and to the clean-up crews. Fire Chief Kim Kercewich laughed:

> The first couple of days, I walked around with a turnout coat on that says "Chief - Alstead", and every time you turned around, there was a reporter there. Okay, so we did away with the bumper coat. Then I went to the vest so that the people who knew that I had an orange vest, like one of those over there, that says "Instant Commander" on it, knew that I was the one to go to. Well, it didn't take too long for the press to figure that out. So I wound up going out with the building inspectors. I put on my forestry hardhat, which is a yellow hardhat like what the power company guys wear, and it was still raining so I put on a yellow raincoat, and I could walk by everyone because they all thought I was working with the power company.

Generally speaking, the people arriving from outside the community were overwhelmingly helpful. "Once people have come, they're still in disbelief and want to give," noted Delvina Kearney. Alstead would need all the help it could get.

The damaged Alstead Village Bridge. *Photograph by Heather Gendron*

Search for the Missing

As that first week wore on, the list of missing persons dropped to a handful. Most of the people who had at one time been listed were discovered in nearby towns or with friends and relatives—fugitives of the flood. One resident, who had left town just before the wave hit, turned up in England. With each passing day, however, hope of finding the four people who remained unaccounted-for dwindled. Thirty people and several dog teams scoured sixteen miles of ravaged and debris-strewn riversides, continuing to search for bodies buried in the rubble.

Bill Seale, a respected local farmer, had been last seen walking quickly away from his home by David Crosby just as the flood wave began to roar down onto Griffin Hill. Unbeknownst to the police, Spencer Petty had been asleep in a camper along the river and had not been warned of the danger posed by the overloaded culvert. Tim and Sally Canfield had simply refused to leave their home when told of the threat.

Even though the discovery would not be released to the public until midweek, the first body was found in a Langdon field as soon as rescue workers began searching the area downstream from Alstead Village on Sunday. It was that of Bill Seale. Although he was nearby, Spencer Petty was not found until Saturday the 15th. Then, on Tuesday and Wednesday of the following week, the bodies of Sally and then Tim Canfield were located along the river in Drewsville, also close together. "We felt better that they were found together so we knew they died together. That was kind of comforting in one way, but not really, in another," said Justin Canfield, on learning what had happened to his aunt and uncle. With the victims found and given proper burials, the town was one step closer to recovery, but there were still many hardships to be overcome.

Search and Rescue. *Photograph by Carol Drummond.*

Search and Rescue workers look for missing persons in the debris. *Photograph by Charlie Brady*

Loss

The death toll in Alstead from the disaster was mercifully small, far smaller than it might have been had not been for the efforts of emergency crews that dark night. The devastation and loss of property was still overwhelming, however. Fifteen homes had been completely washed away. Some families who had lost their houses could not even return to their bare land for it, too, had been washed downstream. More than forty residences were rendered unlivable.

The next four pages are a random selection of some of the most heavily damaged properties along the flood path.

Memorial site for Spencer Petty on Forest Road.
Photograph by Robert Larsen

Memorial for Tim and Sally Canfield at the site of their home which the flood washed away.
Photograph by Heather Gendron

Remains of Bill Seales's home which was completely destroyed on Forest Road.
Photograph by David Crosby

Charlie and Connie Knight's house at 646 Forest Road.
Photograph courtesy of N.H. Department of Safety

Phyllis Duffy's home at foot of Hatch Hill. 639 Forest Road.
Photograph by Dale Guinn

Tom and Sheila Marron's house at 635 Forest Road.
Photograph by Greg Sherwood

Meredith Howard's house at 619 Forest Road.
Photograph by John Fuller

Marty Monahan's property 300 yards below Cooper Hill culvert.
Photograph by Monadnock United Way

Ray and Mary Moore's home at 392 Forest Road.
Photograph by Greg Sherwood

Vera LaFluer's house at 380 Forest Road.
Photograph by Heather Gendron

Stella Winham's property at 366 Forest Road.
Photograph by Greg Sherwood

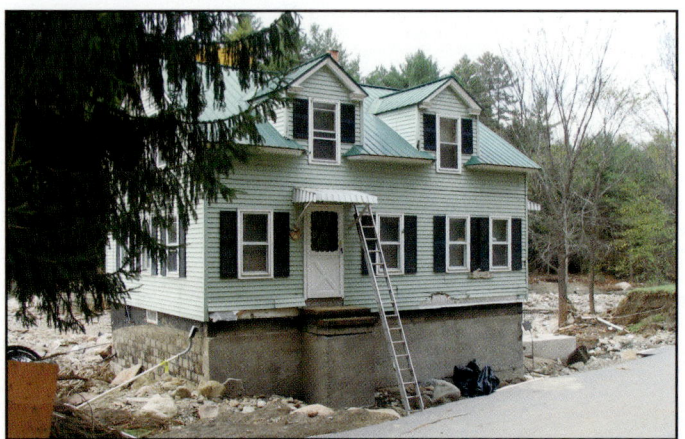
Bobbie and Gene Wilson's house at 356 Forest Road.
Photograph by Heather Gendron

John Sheldon and Annette Newton's house at 313 Forest Road.
Photograph by Stacy Eaton

Allan Parker's house at 260 Forest Road.
Photograph by New Hampshire Department of Safety

Rock and Audrey Wilson's house at 218 Forest Road.
Photograph by Heather Gendron

Jonah and Michelle Gosnell's house at 189 Forest Road.
Photograph by Stacy Eaton

Former Fred Carmen garage, Melody Lane, owned by Joe Bates.
Photograph by Heather Gendron

Joe Bates's property at 115 Forest Road.
Photograph by Stacy Eaton

Linda Pelow's house at 109 Forest Road.
Photograph by David and Julie Hogan

Site of Linda and Kenneth Roller's house at 69 Forest Road.
Photograph by Heather Gendron

Site of Jack Cochrane's house at 47 Forest Road.
Photograph by Heather Gendron

Stanley and Robin Kmiec's house at 15 Forest Road.
Photograph by Patty and Wayne Hatch.

Marx/Wood property at 18 High Street by Alstead Village Bridge.
Photograph by David and Julie Hogan

Blanchflower's Lumber Mill off Library Avenue.
Photograph by Steve Fortier

Site of Marlene and Leroy Wade's home at 133 River Street.
Photograph by Roger Maltby

Fraser and Susan Whitbread's barn from 39 River Street floating by Ramsey's at 145 River Street. *Photograph by Russell Ramsey*

Site of Jeanette Clarks house at 602 Cold River Road, Langdon.
Photograph by Steve Fortier

Upon returning to what was left of their properties, many had a difficult time taking in the magnitude of what had occurred. "We just couldn't believe what we saw: that it took our house and picked it up, foundation and all. It's still not on the ground," Brad Kmiec remembered. "It's still sitting on the back step, the house is," his wife Kitty continued.

> Most of the house floated, but the bathroom, because it was anchored down, didn't, so when we came back, we were like, *Oh good, the house is still standing.* We still have a house, but the more we checked it out, the more we realized it was not salvageable. We realized that the window frames were now cockeyed but the window was straight so you couldn't even open or close the windows anymore. And you walked down the hall and back up the other side, because the house was in a U-shape…Oh, it was a mess; we couldn't even get into the bathroom for a couple days because the bathroom door was wedged shut with mud and debris and whatever floated in the bathroom…so we finally had to break the door off to see what kind of damage had been done in the bathroom. And the cellar—here it is three months later, and we haven't dealt with the cellar yet; it's probably still filled with water and mud because we just haven't

Kitty and Brad Kmiec sort through the rubble from their destroyed house. *Photograph by Bob LaPree, courtesy of* The New Hampshire Union Leader *and UnionLeader.com, October 12, 2005*

gotten around to dealing with it.

    The Red Cross gave us a broom and a mop to clean the house out, but what we needed was a shovel. That's what we did a few months after the flood. We shoveled the floor and threw the mud out the door.

    Brad Kmiec: We found two motorcycle wheels standing upright under the foundation. That is what was holding it up. It basically wasn't repairable, so we gave up on it.

    Kitty: For a long time we thought maybe we can jack it up and try to save it, but we gave up with that idea, and we got a mobile home. We were lucky. I know we lost our house and furniture, but we didn't lose our land. A lot of people lost their land, septic system, well, house, everything…Our land actually sits higher than it did before because there was a lot of fill.

The Kmiec's experience was shared by dozens of other families up and down the river, from directly beneath the Cooper Hill Road culvert all the way down beyond the Drewsville Bridge. Even those who had not completely lost their homes had to cope with damage. "We lost about sixty percent of everything we owned," said Matt Goodell, who had only recently moved into town, and thus still had many things packed in the basement of his home. "All the kids' toys, furniture, camping supplies. Everything that we had ever saved. All our wedding pictures. Everything was completely trashed."

Technician inspects oil tanks at Millot Green.
Photograph by Tafi Brown

Sign from Breshear's Farm Stand.
Photograph by Michael Breshears

Photographs found among flood debris. *Photograph by Don Clark,* The Eagle Times, *October 23, 2005.*

Vehicles gathered from river and stored on Millot Green. *Photograph by Steve Fortier*

Cars piled up on Millot Green. *Photograph by Tafi Brown*

> *They had construction out there for what seemed like forever.*
>
> ~Michaela Gabardi (age 12)

Houses were not the only landmarks that had been lost. As Randy Kmiec put it: "A lot of things that were there are now gone. Like the pond. I used to swim in that all the time. I used to go down to the garage all the time…"

Millot Green at the center of the village, now a muddy field filled with piles of dirt and debris, was also mourned. Justin Canfield recollected:

> I grew up there my entire life. I played baseball there; I played soccer; I played on the basketball courts. To watch that all go away—it's sad…That Millot was built by my family, pretty much. My grandfather donated all those dug-outs, baseball fields we built; we helped seed the grass. We had it all built, and it's all gone now…that was my grandpa and he's not around anymore…that was like the last thing we had left, and now it's gone.

In the days and weeks that followed the flood, displaced families wandered up and down the river valley, scouring the wrecked landscape for any signs of their homes or any belongings that might have remained intact. Some things were easy to locate: cars, piled upon one another; motorcycles smashed into tree trunks; pieces of appliances sticking out of debris piles or impaled through wood. Sharon Perry remembered her own search.

> And the things we couldn't find. We looked everywhere, but there was nothing big. We couldn't find our wood stove or our refrigerator. Ernie's motorcycle was in Bobbie's tree. You couldn't really tell it was a motorcycle. You could only see his decals on it and his manifolds. That hit him really hard. We went looking up there, thinking we had to find something, and we found stupid things like in one of the trees there was…that's my dress. It's like somebody had taken a bunch of clothes right out of the closet and hung them in the tree. They were embedded in the tree, you couldn't even move them. My ski pants that were in a box, they were there for about three weeks, and every time we drive by there are my stupid ski pants stuck on a log. I don't want to see those anymore.
>
> The bride doll that I didn't take, we were down Monday and Ernie bent down behind a log and said, "Is this your doll?" And she was. But she didn't have any clothes on, all her clothes were ripped off. All she had was one little shoe and a piece of lace around her neck. He said 'Do you want this?' Yeah. She's upstairs in a closet wrapped in a towel now. I can't open and shut her eyes because she's full of mud and I don't know how to get the mud out of her head. I tried to take her head off, but I couldn't. I just wanted her to be all cleaned up, but I don't know how to do it.

View of debris on Millot Green. *Photograph by David and Julie Hogan*

Baseball field on Millot Green being used for flood cleanup. *Photograph by Roger Maltby*

Everyone will feel much better when all the wreckage is removed, people rebuild their homes, and the town is once again able to use places like the Millot Green.

~ Alexis Burns -(age 11)

Millot Green should be called Millot Brown.

~ Logan Adams -(age 12)

Contents of Police Station damaged by flood. *Photograph by Steve Fortier*

Arial view of Alstead Village. Millot Green and Alstead Municipal building in upper left. Cold River in foreground. *Photograph courtesy of NH Department of Emergency Planning*

As the initial shock passed, however, most of those who had lost so much realized that they had to go on. No matter how arduous or time-consuming the process, they would rebuild their lives. "I'm sad that I lost my home," reflected Marlene Wade. "I had some beautiful things that I inherited, some beautiful antiques and things, and of course they all went, but you know, they're only things, and you can't build your life on things. There are too many other things that are important."

Cook shack traveled from Millot Green to the Drewsville Bridge. *Photograph by Steve Fortier*

Town Meeting

> *I hope nothing like that ever happens to Alstead or anywhere else again.*
>
> ~ Elizabeth Cubberley (age 11)

Although the residents of Alstead Village eventually were able to pull themselves back onto their feet, confusion, doubt, and growing anger were common in the early days. Emotions boiled to the surface at the town meeting on Tuesday, October 18th. Set up by the selectmen, department chiefs, and representatives of various government agencies, the event was meant to dispel false rumors about the clean-up and to directly answer the questions and concerns of residents. It was held in the small auditorium of Vilas Middle School, and by 7:00 P.M. more than 800 people had come, well exceeding the previous town meeting record of 643.

"It was pretty contentious," remembered Joel McCarty. "A bunch of people were pretty spooked, pretty angry, looking for someone to blame—which, of course, is a common affliction in America." Questions ranged from the safety of the water supply, to the state of the roads in and out of town, to when schools would reopen, to when federal disaster aid would arrive for afflicted families and individuals. Few things had been decided by that night, and many people remained unsatisfied with the answers they had received; doubt and anger still hung heavily in the air.

As time wore on and bills began to pile up, some of the most frequent complaints were about FEMA. The Federal Emergency Management Agency, overtaxed by the disastrous Hurricane Katrina in the Gulf Coast, was sometimes resented for the modest compensation the agency eventually was able to give out. Ruined homeowners who were initially hopeful when a FEMA inspector came by to assess each damaged property became dissatisfied when their relief checks finally came. Some families who had lost everything received less than a thousand dollars, and they didn't see any of it for months. "I'm really not thrilled with FEMA," said Linda Anderson. "I'm glad that the town of Alstead has been sending checks periodically because that's really helping to get me back on my feet."

Much of the dissatisfaction with the agency stemmed from exaggerated expectations. "FEMA does not swoop in and make it all better," said Matt Saxton. "FEMA came in and people were furious or crushed by what they heard, but FEMA acted as it is statutorily set out to act. It did all that it could, based on what it is designed to do." As Jan Howe observed, "They were concerned and caring people, but they did have limited mandates."

The Town Recovers

When a town is torn in half, patched together, left to find its old identity in piles of debris, what happens to those who are neither the victims nor the heroes? In many cases they leave themselves out of the story altogether. When asked what the worst part of the flood was, Dylan Martin (age 7), son of firefighter Don Martin, answered, "I don't know, but my Dad does." His response mirrors the reactions of so many Alstead residents, dismissing their own losses in the context of greater loss, and their minor hardships in the face of tragedy. Yet even the little things have their significance, and the responses of the children, the fate of the animals, and residents' everyday inconveniences are as much a part of the story as the wall of water that ripped through the village.

The Animals

"Don't forget about animals," twelve-year-old Chris French wrote. "They were victims as well, and they could have been washed away too, especially wild animals." Fortunately, pets were rarely forgotten. Dogs and cats were brought to the fire station on Saturday night with their anxious owners. In some cases—as in the Hilow family's situation—the search for frightened pets dangerously slowed the process of evacuating. For all their owners' care, some animals were lost. Nine year old Christie Fish had an unfortunate surprise awaiting her: "When I got home…my cat died because of the flood."

Some animals were surprisingly resilient. Angela Hilow remembers returning to her property on Sunday morning and looking at the remnants of her neighbor's house. "They had a chunk of their house left…and their dog was there hanging on the back of the

Overleaf:
Zev Kazati-Morgan walks on road at Hatch Hill.
Photograph by Kate Tarlow Morgan

Meredith Howard's dog at the library for an interview.
Photograph by David Moody

couch…he survived." For some animals who managed to escape, they returned to find their old homes had disappeared and their owners gone. Needless to say, some residents have adopted several cats—refugees of the flood. Fortunately, not only were there people willing to take the animals in, but there were gifts to help feed them. Mary Lou Huffling remembers, "Karen, the manager at Agway in Walpole contacted the pet food salesmen, and we got a couple of trailer loads of Science Diet for Dogs and Kitties. They pulled it all the way from the Mid-West!"

That's My Dog!
as told by Eleanor Elbers

On Sunday morning when everyone walked down to the falls—or at least we had…they came back, and they said "Moe almost died!"

I asked, "What happened?"

There is a millpond there on Route 123. There is the mill and there are the mill falls that power the mill, which usually doesn't have a lot of power in it, but this day it was rushing through. The water was bashing up against the mill, almost up to the windows. This is four feet up, just pounding.

So Moe jumped in on the far side of the millpond. He was sucked under the road, under the culvert. He came out on the other side of the road…up out of the culvert; he comes out on the side where the mill is; he's bashed up against it. The water throws him up against the mill and he is scraping, trying to get out, and my friends who had come down are crying "Oh god, Anton's dog is dying in the middle of the river! What are we going to tell him? Oh, no!"

And then he pitches over this waterfall that was very powerfully running and bashes his head on a tree in the middle of it, bashes his head on the tree and then just floats down the river. So Marty says, "Oh god! I had better go find the body." So he…walks down the hill, and Moe just comes trotting back up—300 to 400 yards down!

So…the next morning the news people come tearing in, and they're clamoring, "We need a story. We can't get into the village." …[Anton] told them the story, and it got on the news. It was all over the country and even on Honduran television! One of our daughters, a Fall Mountain [High School] graduate, was in a bar. She's in the Peace Corps in Honduras in Catacalas. She was in a bar or a hotel or someplace, and she's walking through. They have the television on CNN news. It says,

"Flooding in Alstead: Pooch Rescued!"

And she's like, "Wait a minute, wait a minute! That's my dog!"

Floodwaters receding at Chase's Mill, late on October 9. *Photograph by Nicholas Brown*

The Children

> These children are the next generation…of this town. They're the ones who will be retelling [this story] to their children who didn't experience it. You know, they can sit now with their grandparents and experience it, but when they become grandparents one day, their little ones will say, "Grandma, tell me about that time you got all that rain."
>
> *Courtney Porter*

As long as they are safe and healthy, children are often overlooked in the aftermath of disaster, even by their parents. "You could tell that the last thing they had time for—or even were thinking about—was their kids," Courtney Porter remembers, "not because they're bad parents, but because they have so much going on." Even if they were disregarded amidst the frantic activity of clean-up and immediate relief, the children's reactions are still significant. In some ways their responses were less ambiguous expressions of the same emotions that flooded the adult world—the awe, the fear, the sense of loss of material possessions, the need to gawk, and in some cases, empathy with those who suffered.

Many children lost all their toys and possessions in the flood.
Photograph by John and Hazel Fuller

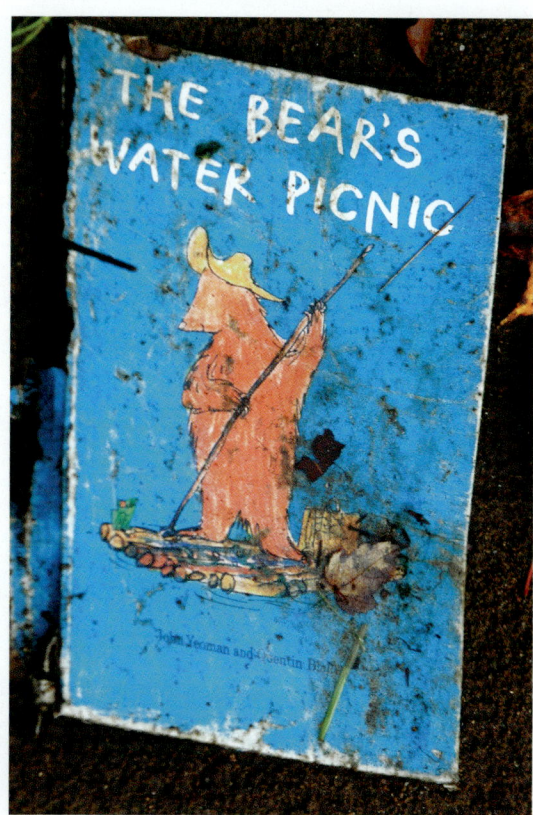
Book found in the flood debris.
Photograph by Stacy Eaton

Courtney Porter's children expressed two quite different emotions. While Courtney was stranded in East Alstead, incapable of returning to her home on Main Street, eleven-year-old Andrea was at a relative's horse farm and six-year-old Cade was staying with family in Acworth. Courtney, who was related by marriage to the Canfields, had a difficult responsibility: "I needed to explain to my children, 'Your aunt and uncle are missing.'" Her daughter Andrea was concerned and wanted to come home immediately to see how everyone was doing. Cade, on the other hand, was too amazed to be upset: "Oh Mom, you should see what it looks like!" he told Courtney after spending the day searching for his missing aunt and uncle. When the National Guard arrived, it was one more novelty: "The army guys are everywhere!" Courtney was not so thrilled: "I mean, it's great. I'm so thankful that the National Guard is here, that they're helping us, but it's one of those things that—especially for a six-year-old boy—you don't know exactly how he's taking it in…and he's like, 'Wow, it's cool,' …and I'm trying to explain to him, 'It's good that they're here, but it's not cool.' "

Just as the tangible novelty of the flood was a thrill for Cade, so too did the material world become a cause of sorrow for children in the flood's path. In a joint interview of two nine-year-old girls, one bemoaned the loss of her toys moments after the other was speaking of the death of a relative. Courtney remembers talking to one boy who had lost his house, and he too said: "I lost all my toys!"—a child's equivalent of "everything I owned."

There were also moments when the children displayed remarkable insight. Courtney remembers one girl in particular:

> Katie…she's three, and I remember one of the first times it rained after the flood, I remember her coming to school and saying, "I hate it when it rains!"…I remember thinking, for children dealing with this—and even for adults—making that whole correlation between rain and the bad things that happened, I said, "Oh, come here, come here, I hate the rain, too!"

Talking about the flood strengthened the understanding of many of the children, Eleanor Elbers observed. "These conversations got really mature, really fast. You always hear how disaster makes children grow up really quickly." This presented a danger that Eleanor was well aware of: "I don't want them to grow up in a way where they get hardened or cut off."

The Jack-O'-Lantern
by Karyn Kaminski

The day after the flood our family took a walk from Cobb Hill to the intersection of Routes 12A and 123 (Forest Road). We returned home feeling shocked and saddened by the devastation we saw. To lift our spirits, we decided to carve pumpkins. My five-year-old, Russell, expressed his sadness through pumpkin carving. He was insistent that his pumpkin have a frown with one tooth and no eyes. Although he did not verbalize it, this was his way of telling us that he did not like what he had seen and was quite saddened by it.

To keep that from happening, the children needed a safe place to be, companionship, and an opportunity to express their emotions and be sensitive to the emotions of others. Where could they find such a place? Many parents were too frazzled and preoccupied to be as supportive as they would have liked. The public schools were closed. Fortunately, Eleanor was thinking ahead.

"The next morning, I just said, Well, I am going down to The Orchard School to see what happens." She called the state to make sure her plans were legal, and was given a confident: Do what you have to do. Courtney Porter, meanwhile, was still stranded in East Alstead—a fortunate thing since she had been a teacher at the Orchard School for six years.

She remembers that Monday morning: "We just started calling, getting on cell phones and letting families know that we were here: if they could get here, we would be here." Of course, with the ever-changing landscape of passable roads, it was complicated for many parents to bring their children to East Alstead. Roads would be declared open, and parents would drive that way only to find them closed. In some cases, they would be opened in the morning and then under construction again when parents came back to pick up their kids. Courtney thought that "The hardest thing, I think, was parents just figuring out how to get here. Once people were here, it was great!"

Twelve children from ages three to eleven showed up on the first day. "To run a school when no other schools were open was pretty amazing," said Courtney. The mixing of school-aged children with the usual preschoolers added its own element to the experience,

When we finally got back to school, everyone talked about their experiences.

~ Jamie MacDonald (age 12)

Rain falling on a broken Alstead Road. "There is a crack in the road so they put cones up to block it off. We went on the side of the road. It wasn't safe." *Watercolor and crayon painting by Erica Page (age 5)*

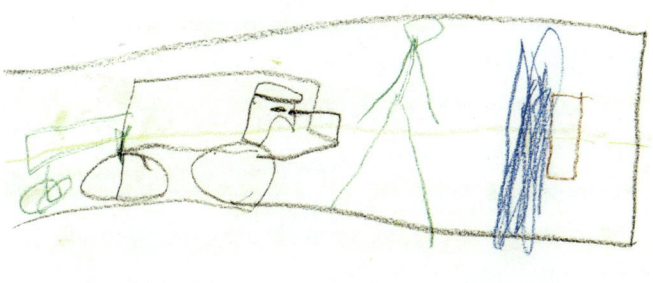

"I was with my parents and there was a big log in the road. Someone had to get the fire department. My parents are the fire department. There is more fire department coming and my dad is walking out and he needs help!" *Crayon drawing by Devin Olmstead (age 5)*

recalls Eleanor. "A lot of mixed-aged children generally…will turn into that family unit where kids are counseling each other, and the younger kids were bringing the older kids out of seriousness." During that first day, they sang songs about floods, read books about floods, and drew pictures of what they had seen, while the teachers assessed the situation to determine how they could make it through the week.

By the following day, Eleanor had created a Flood Curriculum to bolster the support they were offering the children. She set up separate corners of the room devoted to drawing and painting, reading, and pretending. "Each child had a different need," she remembers. By tapping into these needs, according to Courtney, they created "an outlet for their confusion, their stress, their anger, their questions…We wrote, they painted, we talked, just reenacting the feelings that they had…" Eleanor remembers, "There was no place they would rather be. They didn't want to be home in the chaos: they just wanted to be at school."

Georgia and Jacy

[An e-mail from Doris Bittenbender to Peggy Bittenbender] December 3rd, 2005

Hi Peggy,

I just wanted to keep you informed when I hear the girls talking about the flood. Didn't have a chance to tell you before I left on Wednesday. Probably you see this kind of play all the time, but I don't want to forget to mention it.

When G & J were playing upstairs I was the mom and they were the sisters. At one point Georgia decided to "tidy up" the room (which was the "house") and they started making beds and folding blankets…I figured this would take a while so I went downstairs to check on the muffins. I came back up in about 10 minutes, at which time they told me that now the room was a hotel where we had had to move because of the flood. "The police came and knocked on our door. They told us to leave but we didn't. Then the water started to come and we decided to leave so we were okay. The flood came from a river that is usually small but got very big. It broke the house into pieces and they all went down the river. So now we are living in this hotel." The explanation that I have put in quotes was said by both of them, sort of overlapping.

They were happy in their play, not anxious, just matter-of-fact. I am not telling you this because I am alarmed. I think it is probably healthy that they talk and play about the flood rather than bottle it up. I just like to let you know. They are such happy girls. I doubt they are lying awake nights with fears about the flood, but it seems to be very much a part of their thoughts…

Doris

Meanwhile, the school was providing support for the parents. "We also gave some tools and resources to the families," Courtney says, "because I think a lot of times in situations like this, the adults are working so hard on the situation itself that it's very easy to forget that they have children, too, who are being affected by this. So we gave parents space and time." They occasionally gave advice as well:

> There was an earthquake at the time, but it looked like there was a flood—over in the Philippines, I think. So we had children coming to us with such confusion: "I heard that down in the village a school has collapsed and there's fifty children stuck under it!" It's one of those things—having to really talk to parents and say, "You have to shut the TV off! Your children are in a state of shock right now and are getting mixed signals about disasters happening."

Perhaps the best thing for the parents was knowing they could do what they had to do, and their children were in a good place. "When you get parents together who have been struggling, and when at the end of the day you see a mom or a dad who's just so drained, and then their kid comes running to them…" Courtney chokes at the recollection, "and to see the look—you know we're doing good things here."

Boy assists with cleaning up flood debris.
Photograph by Paul Garcia

"Where there was a gas station, there is now a river. And there is gas and oil all around there. It's polluted. Why don't they build something that makes it not pollute the river? Someone better not put a cigarette in there. It would make a fire and explosion." *Drawing by Emma Berg (age 10)*

> *Having fun with my friends made me feel better about what happened to Alstead.*
>
> *~ Mary Locke (age 12)*

Those kids who didn't go to The Orchard School were out of school for more than a week. The roads were in such disarray that it would have been impossible for buses to bring everyone to school both in Alstead and in the Fall Mountain Regional School District as a whole. Sixth-grader Jamie MacDonald explained the situation:

> Since there was no power and no phone lines, we had no school for the whole district for a week. Then everyone except Vilas Middle School and Alstead Primary went back to school…because the National Guard was staying in Vilas's gym and there was no bridge on one side, and the other bridge was too weak for lots of traffic to go over. No school was boring.

Jamie wasn't the only one who needed something to do. "I was very bored because I didn't have anyone to play with," eleven-year-old Grace Rushing wrote. Sixth-grader Sabrina Sodders agreed: "Kids were tired of reading books and magazines, bored all day and all night with nothing to do."

Some students, however, never had a chance to get bored. Twins Derek and Jesse Sherburne, both juniors in high school, finished pumping their own basement and spent the rest of

Kindernook preschool children get a hayride in an articulated haul truck. *Photograph by Erin Heidorn*

the week at Scott and Wendy Gendron's house. "We were helping them shovel three feet of mud out of their basement, helping them collect family possessions…so we were busy." When they were not working, they were "trying to stay fueled, getting ready for the next day, getting stuff together, getting clothes clean." That was a health precaution when working with flood debris—a mysterious mixture of household possessions, mud, gasoline, sewage, and whatever else might have been upstream. Yet Derek and Jesse, far from complaining about the working conditions, were eager to help their friends "get back on their feet." Their only personal regrets: Derek had injured his arm and Jesse his thumb in recent football games, slowing down their mud-removal rate. "I wish I could have been a hundred percent," Jesse says.

When road agent David Crosby came home on Monday, he found his son Jarid busy: "He had my tractor and he was building a road from my house up to the class six road that runs from Kmiec's to Cobb Hill. He got that road built so my brother could get out, my Mom and Dad could get in and out to Grammie…he's eleven years old." With the help of the tractor, Jarid brought in dirt, smoothed it out, cut trees and brush where needed, and pushed obstacles out of the way. "That is what I've taught him," David stated with pride.

For some students—at least those whose fathers weren't road agents—the week off from school was an unexpected opportunity to play. With power outages making TVs and computers useless, play sometimes took on an old-fashioned twist. "We played lots of board games. We couldn't watch TV or play video games, so we played outside," remembers eight-year-old Dylan Plaistead, who decided that that was, in fact, more fun than his electronic amusements.

Despite the initial appeal of a surprise vacation, many students were anxious to get back to school. "I was…worried about the school," eleven-year-old Grace Rushing recalls, "I like Alstead, and I was hoping the school was okay. I may not like homework, but I like school very much. It is not nice to see the school closed." When school resumed on Wednesday, it was a relief for many. "It felt better," said Dylan Martin of his first day back, although his usual seventeen-minute bus ride had almost doubled. For many, seeing friends was worth the extra drive. "When we finally got back to school, everyone talked about their experiences," wrote Jamie MacDonald. Some classmates had experienced the flood first-hand, he remembers; others still did not know what was happening.

> *The stores are open again and we kids are going back to school. Now, everything is great.*
>
> *~ Paige O'Dette (age 12)*

> *Now people wished that this never happened because they wanted to go back to their old houses, old beds, and old lives. All they can do is wish, because it will never happen.*
>
> *~ Lauren Ramsey (age 11)*

The school also became an eagerly-awaited destination when October 31st arrived. "The roads weren't safe enough for trick-or-treating," Bradley Gordon remembers "so volunteers planned a giant Halloween party in the school's gym."

Four days later, another festivity was underway. It was Luke Nelson's seventh birthday, but since he lived at the foot of Hatch Hill, his mom Diana Nelson remembers, "He was worried that his friends wouldn't come visit anymore…but they all came. They came all different ways: down Cobb Hill; some tried to come down Hatch Hill and had to go back and around; they came through Acworth. They worked so hard to come. Luke was pleased." For Luke, at least, things were almost back to normal.

Fourth-grade class from Vilas Primary School visits Gov. Lynch in Concord.
Photograph by teacher Judy Checchi

Everyday Inconveniences

When the power went out a little after seven o'clock on a Sunday morning, most people didn't think too much of it. With so many trees crowding the power lines that paralleled area roads, it was not uncommon to temporarily lose electricity because of some windstorm, snowstorm, or rainstorm as the case may be. But the telephones dead? That rarely happened. Even residents who lived far from the center of destruction felt that something was wrong.

Without telephones, without power to run the radio or television, and the washed-out roads leaving so many areas inaccessible, information was slow in traveling. "The first thing I wanted to do was to find out what was really happening, and there was no way to get the news," says Eleanor Elbers. " I just realized how our culture is…information obsessed!" There were other consequences as well.

On the Monday after the flooding, a man on Route 123 suffered a heart attack. Without phone service, and unaware that the East Alstead fire-station was now staffed, his wife drove ten minutes to Marlow to call 911. By the time the ambulance reached him, it was too late. "I don't know if in his condition it would have made a difference," Anton Elbers stated, "but it definitely impressed the importance of getting out and letting this area know there was twenty-four hour coverage at the fire station."

If information had stopped flowing in Alstead, nothing of the sort had happened in the rest of the world. When her phone service was restored, Eleanor had a surprise waiting for her:

Water use restrictions in Alstead Municipal Office restroom.
Photograph by David Moody

> I had thirty-five calls on my answering machine…when I actually got to the phone. It took me an hour to listen to all these messages, which were from people who had seen Moe [the Elbers's dog] on television or heard about it. There was a message from [my daughter in Honduras], a message from a person we had lived with in Alstead thirty-four years ago. And [a friend] who lives in California…I was getting calls from people all over trying to reach us—of course, my mom, my brother, people I hadn't heard from for years. One asked, "Are you guys alive?"—that was the most interesting one.

Lorraine Dustin remembers calls from California, Florida, the Carolinas, and Tennessee. Chief Lyons marveled at Alstead's sudden fame: "A lot of people didn't even know where Alstead was until this happened." Dale Dustin agreed. "It definitely put Alstead on the map, not for a good reason, but it definitely put Alstead on the map."

In one place, there was a 20-40 ft. drop-off!

~Jered Smith (age 12)

Yet the Alstead being broadcast nationally and internationally was far from the Alstead that people had known for years. With whole stretches of the town demolished and hundreds of trucks crawling across the devastated landscape, "it was like you were in a war zone!" Sherry Stanley exclaimed. By Monday, the effect was heightened by the arrival of the National Guard. "You get a sense of *Omigod!*" says Delvina Kearney. Because they may have come from areas where strict regulations are necessary, Delvina was concerned that they might misunderstand Alstead. "You know, this town isn't like any other town. This town is a small community. You don't need guns. You don't need anything. All you need to do is talk to people." The military presence, as much as it provided a sense of order in a time of chaos, had another effect: "It was also a sense of fear that they instilled at first, because when you're in uniform…it's intimidating…they're in control."

Also, there were rules. "I didn't always hear about [them], but there were curfews at nighttime," Delvina recalls. "People were told that after seven o'clock they weren't allowed to be out." David and Jeanne Moody were driving home at about nine o'clock when a National Guardsman pulled them over and asked why they weren't respecting the curfew.

"What curfew?" they asked.

"The one that was announced on television," the guard replied.

The end of Cooper Hill Road where it intersects Forest Road. *Photograph by Greg Sherwood*

When Jeanne brought up the fact that they—like almost everyone in Alstead—had no power and therefore no way of knowing what regulations were announced in this fashion, the guard shrugged amiably: "Someone didn't think this through."

Fortunately, some rules were thought through. To protect the damaged bridge in the Alstead Village, residents had to use special orange passes. The Guard controlled the flow of traffic in and out of town as well, with checkpoints to help minimize nonresidents' contribution to the chaos. "It was a horrible sense for two weeks," Delvina remembers. "'Who are you? What are you doing? You can only come in if you work here.'"

Driving in and out of town was difficult even without the interference of the National Guard. On Sunday, when Linda Putnam was attempting to return from Massachusetts to her home on North Road, she stopped at the McDonalds restaurant in Hillsborough to get more information. "You can't get there from here," they told her, "and we're not sure you can get there from anywhere else." Fortunately, Linda was familiar with the back roads, so she did make it home—two and a half hours later. The next day she decided to check on relatives. "We have always considered ourselves lucky to live so close to our families," she wrote, but in the aftermath of the flood, it was not an advantage.

> My parents live on River Street, and my sister lives on Murphy Hill, usually just a ten minute drive from our home. One and a half hours, and fifty-five miles later, we made it to Murphy Hill. In order to check on my parents we added another forty-five minutes and twenty-one miles. My sister had spoken to my dad from different sides of the river earlier that morning. But for me to hear their story firsthand, I had to drive seventy-six miles.

This lack of mobility posed a serious threat to local businesses like Delvina's general store. "For me, my business thrived on Acworth, people from [Route]123…but however you usually came to Alstead, you couldn't come in, so I was thinking, *How am I going to survive?* What I sold most of when the Guard was here was soda, cigarettes, coffee, and it was like my whole purpose for two weeks." Though she worked twelve-hour days, offering comfort and security to residents, her business suffered: "I didn't make any money. I can't compete with the Red Cross, the Salvation Army, Wal-Mart coming in with so much food…It was pretty scary: *Am I going to survive? Can I stay in business?*"

For all the hardships and inconveniences for Alstead residents, there were some heartening surprises. "We were expecting people to be falling in holes and breaking legs and that kind

When everyone tried to help out, the town pulled itself together.

~ Bradley Gordon (age 11)

of thing because so many people were out wandering about," remembers Anton Elbers. "There were a lot of places where the road had dropouts of four feet or more, places where the road was undermined." But somehow, for all the walking and climbing and hiking, "things were pretty quiet."

In general, things were pretty quiet—perhaps all the more quiet after the roar of rain and rushing water that preceded the silence. Eleanor Elbers was almost wistful as she remembers those first few days after the flood.

> There was a lot of kind of wonderful, strange time. You know, I shouldn't say wonderful when people lost everything, but definitely a time with a lot of connection…people were just walking by at night with nothing else to do. I've always loved that about living simply and not having a television and stuff…There was just this welcome, because you couldn't drive places too easily, and it was very still and quiet. It reminded me of being in Honduras…There's just a kind of freedom from time; it was kind of wonderful.

Although much of Alstead had reverted to a preindustrial pace of life, the rest of the world rushed on. Even Eleanor admitted, "It would have been hard to keep up." Adults had to go work, students to school, and customers to the shops. The fractured infrastructure that had strewn the town with third-world charm also presented barriers between residents and these everyday occupations—barriers of torn-up tar and splintered trees. As shaken residents craved a sense of normalcy, it was clear: these barriers had to be removed as quickly as possible.

Alstead's first traffic light ever at the temporary one-lane section of Forest Road.. *Photograph by Steve Fortier.*

Rebuilding

Now we are rebuilding Alstead in hope of a new beginning.

~ Cassidy Morse (age 11)

Overleaf: Exposed ledge along narrow portion of Warren Brook. Photograph by Mike Wright

In the days following the flood, Alstead was all but cut off from the outside world. The only way into Alstead Village from neighboring Charlestown or Acworth was on winding Langdon roads. From Keene or Walpole, people had to first go through Drewsville and then take Hill Road into town, or a similar variation. Once in the the village, it was an ordeal to reach East Alstead. According to Chief Lyons, residents and workers had to go "down the street to Drewsville, Route 12, go across Route 9, come up Gilsum Mine Road off of [Route] 10—that's the only physical way that you can get to the other side of town, and that's an hour's ride." Therefore, before any real reconstruction could begin, the basic infrastructure had to be reestablished.

As the town Highway Department and various state departments—the New Hampshire Department of Transportation (NHDOT), the Highway Maintenance Bureau, and the Bridge and Maintenance Bureau—rushed to begin work, they faced a daunting landscape. "In some areas, the stream channel had been rerouted to where the road originally existed," wrote Richard Lane.[24] "Other areas were buried under assorted debris and soil deposits with boulders (three to four feet in diameter)." Telephone wires were tangled amidst the wreckage; five miles of utility poles were down on Route 123 alone. Piles of debris clogged the area and needed to be searched and removed. Despite these circumstances, the bulk of the work had to be completed before winter set in.

Repairs proceed on Alstead Village Bridge. *Photograph by David Collins*

Where to Start?

"You had to start from the center of the town and work your way to the outside, because there was no way to work in to you," explained David Crosby, who was responsible for rebuilding the town roads. The Town Barn, with the road equipment and the town's fuel supply, was cut off from the village. By building out, much-needed materials and equipment could flow to the reconstruction sites.

As David started work on the town roads, Craig Forrest, NHDOT Contract Administrator, came to a similar conclusion on rebuilding the state roads. "It was kind of hard to figure out where to start, and the best place to start. To be honest with you, I think I never saw the whole site until probably the end of that first week." Yet he soon decided that the Drewsville Bridge would be the best place to begin. Cold River Material with its sand and gravel quarries would then be accessible to the rest of the town.

Unlike David who was responsible for his own roads, Craig's situation posed a complication. As a state department, NHDOT decisions are customarily made at the headquarters in Concord. Yet the time it would take to shuffle through the official bureaucracy and go through the usual rebuilding processes could have become a major setback. "Actually in this case," Craig remembers, "things moved along pretty quickly. The governor stepped in right from the beginning and said, "Do whatever it takes." They would figure the details about how to make payments, but they wanted the work to start as soon as it could." The NHDOT signed a contract with Frank Whitcomb Construction, a local company that had, coincidentally, just been working on a flood repair project in the nearby town of Westmoreland. With a go-ahead from Transportation Commissioner Carol Murray on the day after the flood, reconstruction began without delay.

When the flood ruined some yards, it also destroyed wells.

~Daniel Zoilkowski (age 12)

Truck carries crushed rock to repair Drewsville Bridge. *Photograph by Randy Rhoades*

> *The hard part is going to be getting to school - a polluted river is right in the way!*
>
> *~ Emma Berg (age 10)*

The Work

"This is the first time I've ever had to work in this capacity," said Rick Oberst, an NHDOT contract administrator working with Craig Forrest. The vast scale of the destruction, the initial inaccessibility of resources, the unexpected nature of the construction, the plethora of outside pressures—all these obstacles transformed the project into a daunting task.

Although as a former manager at Whitcomb Construction, David Crosby was in his element, he was far from comfortable. "I was used to having to go a hundred different directions at once…[but] there were some times when I couldn't get from one crew to the next, and they had to wait an hour or two before I got them onto another job—there were not enough of us to go around." With so many volunteers and businesses working together, David's job as coordinator became increasingly difficult:

> We were calling in help from everywhere at that point. There was almost too much help; you couldn't handle it all, you know, being one person. You just couldn't keep track of everything, and I knew I had to keep everything documented for our paperwork, because I knew FEMA's going to have to come in here, so I've got to keep on top of all this paperwork…
>
> If you have one contractor working on one job, it's a piece of cake, but if you have five contractors working in five different places trying to put things back together—there's only one of me.

Burning debris on Forest Road. *Photograph by Stacy Eaton*

As Whitcomb and other contractors were working repairing roads, Eastern Logging was in charge of debris removal—all working as quickly as possible. In many cases the National Guard's presence compounded David's problem. "They're not from here. They don't know where anything is and don't know where to go with it, so I pretty much had to take them by the hand and lead them from this spot to that spot—and I didn't have time to do that." In many cases, "It was a nightmare."

It was a pleasant change when helpers came in who didn't need as much guidance. "The local guys knew right where to go, right what to do," David recalls. Firefighter Donna Olmstead remembers the selfless spirit of local volunteers: "You'd ask, 'Can you do this?' and it might be the worst job in the world, and they'd say, 'Fine.'" In many cases, workers even risked their own lives to help out. To get from one side of the village to the other, workers had to cross the bridge that had been buffeted by debris and floodwaters, everyone knew it was unstable and at first, public traffic was prevented from crossing. For the workers, it was another story. "Everyone said, 'Don't cross the bridge,'" David Crosby recalled, "and everyone crossed the bridge."

The US Natural Resources Conservation Service (NRCS) staff presents a check for funding erosion control projects to the Alstead selectmen. Far left: Bill Moran. Center: Joel McCarty. Far Right: Matt Saxton.
Photograph courtesy of NRCS

Burning debris on the banks of the Cold River. *Photograph by Don Clark, courtesy of* The Eagle Times, *November 20, 2005*

Humanity In Concord

It is very easy to be cynical about government. I can't be anymore, not about state government. We found humanity in Concord, which is all that we asked for—all that we needed—and we found it.[25]

Matt Saxton

Governor John Lynch was flying to Europe on a trade mission on Saturday, October 8th when he received word of flooding in New Hampshire. Switching course, he returned home, and by five o'clock on Sunday morning, he declared a state of emergency.[26] Soon he was surveying the disaster firsthand with other elected officials, including U.S. Senators Judd Gregg and John Sununu and U.S. Representative Charlie Bass.[27]

"The reason I'm here," Governor Lynch explained to the *New Hampshire Union Leader*, "is to identify problems and find solutions."[28] Lynch traveled back and forth between Concord, Alstead and other flooded towns, to oversee relief and repairs. Though national funding would take weeks to arrive, he urged local officials and state departments to begin reconstruction as soon as possible. "I'd say go forward and not wait on FEMA. I think repairs should be made now because winter will be here before you know it."[29] By October 26th, President George W. Bush declared the flooding in the Monadnock region a major natural disaster, and soon national relief was provided to the region. In spring, Concord came through once again. With Governor Lynch's backing and nearly unanimous congressional support, two bills were passed to assist in the recovery process—one to finance reconstruction efforts, and another to buy-out devastated properties.

In addition to securing funding, Lynch and other politicians comforted residents with their more human side. "He's been here five times," Matt Saxton reported of Governor Lynch nine days after the disaster. "He is totally sincere in his desire to make Alstead whole. This support has helped us a great deal." From the very beginning, Lynch told reporters that his first priority was the health and safety of residents.[30] He even handed out laminated cards with his phone number in case people needed assistance. He explained, "I want the families to be treated just as if they were my own family."[31]

Governor John Lynch signs the "Buy-out bill" into law. at the Alstead Town Hall. Behind the governor left to right: State Rep. Daniel Eaton, State Sen. Bob Odell, Annette Newton, Rep. Sheldon Sawyer (Walpole), Alstead Selectman Matthew Saxton, Rep. Jack Pratt (Walpole), Rep. Jay Phinizy (Acworth), Martha Cooper, Rep. Deborah Hogancamp (Chesterfield), Rep. Henry Parkhurst (Winchester).
Photograph by Tafi Brown

Meanwhile, Craig Forest and Rick Oberst were working with forty to fifty other people, and cooperation was essential. "We didn't go out there and say, 'Do this. Do that,'" said Craig. "We all worked together. Even the contractor would come up with recommendations and we would say yes or no." Unlike standard NHDOT projects that are designed by specialists in Concord, emergency work demanded a much quicker design process. It was often done in the field as the workers built the foundations, using their own experience to determine where to add drainage pipes. This required collaboration, not only between coordinators like Craig and the designers from Concord, but also with residents whose familiarity with the old roads helped ensure they were rebuilt in a similar fashion. According to Craig the level of cooperation and flexibility was incredible. "I think everyone realized that it was emergency work. It had to be done."

Around the Clock

"Oh, yes," Craig Forest responded immediately when asked if he felt pressure. "You were constantly thinking, *It's going to get cold soon, and you have to get things closed up before the weather gets bad.*" If left to their own devices, the amount of work for the road crews was daunting, but external pressures compounded the problem.

Trucks haul road fill along Forest Road. *Photograph by Stacy Eaton*

I haven't seen my mom and dad much, but I saw them on TV!

~ Alex Kercewich (age 5)

The hard part was we had no electricity for awhile, but the good part is there's more light now.

~ Zev Kazati-Morgan (age 5)

"Every agency had its directors, and coordination at times was difficult," Rick Oberst added, "as there were so many parties involved." Craig Forest elaborated on the situation:

> It was difficult because, of course, we were trying to rebuild the roads, but the governor's big push was to get the utilities—power and telephone—back to the residents who were still there, so basically, what we had to do was to try to get a road through that could be passed by utility companies, and so we had to coordinate our work with them. And then, of course… residents started coming back to their homes so they were there, and then we had the debris cleanup people, too… There were a lot of people trying to work in the same area, so that got confusing sometimes.

As Craig observed, the residents themselves presented a problem. Rick remembers, "As soon as there was any semblance of a path…people started driving, and it made it difficult to continue with the construction." Although they would have liked to raise the road to a certain level and put in appropriate drainage, this was often difficult with a public eager to get through. "By no means had [a road] been completed, when people were using it. It was sometimes frustrating, but I think everyone understood everyone's need to get in there and see what was going on…to see what was happening to their property."

With so many pressures, everyone was working long hours. "We went a lot of days without a day off," Craig remembers, "so one day sort of turned into the next. We'd go home, have something to eat, catch a little sleep and go back." On that schedule, things moved quickly. A rough road was built to the Town Barn by late Tuesday or Wednesday. The Drewsville

Telephone and electrical utility trucks line up on Forest Road. *Photograph by David Collins*

Bridge took only about a week to get back into operation. Alstead's highway crews managed to get all their roads ready for winter in six weeks. According to Craig, Route 123A was passable sometime in November, but they had some finishing-work to do before it was open to the public. "When we were there working in December," Craig remembers, "it was probably the coldest part of the winter…and after we were finished it warmed up!" Yet right before Christmas, they had most things back where they needed to be.

"They did a beautiful job," said Police Chief Lyons. Lorraine Dustin agreed. "They have worked around the clock on the roads around here and they have done beautifully." When Route 12A officially opened the Friday before Christmas, Lorraine was excited. "I just couldn't wait to travel that road again because the other way is so steep…I feel much more comfortable coming down the other way." The Larsens were grateful for the one-lane road that was put in a little way above Kmiec's on Forest Road (Route 123). The four-mile round trip to the village had become a twelve-mile round trip after the flood. "It was just amazing the amount of work that took place in a short period of time," said Mary Larsen. Her husband Bob added, "They were working twenty-four hours a day, seven days a week."

But the job was not done yet. In fact, much of what was done will have to be ripped up so that the road can be rebuilt according to a more carefully planned design and upgraded to current standards. While Craig's attention has shifted to paperwork—the layers of bureaucracy that he had so luckily bypassed earlier in the project—the NHDOT has been designing the new road. Though it may be too early to say, Alstead's residents may soon have much better roads and newer utilities than they had before the flood.

I think next time there is a flood warning, Alstead members will react differently.

~ Kevin Plummer (age 12)

Excavator gathers debris in the Cold River.
Photograph by Mike Heidorn

Workers survey Cold River debris fields.
Photograph by David Hogan

Water quality sampling to evaluate effects of the flood. *Photograph by Mike Heidorn*

Millot Green's loam being sifted prior to reconstruction of the park. *Photograph by David Moody*

How Much Did It Cost?

Selectman Joel McCarty had to accept many unknowns when trying to assess the financial aspects of the flood:

> Our budget didn't actually change from one year to the next, but we got $700,000 from FEMA that we spent on the roads. We're putting in a new well today because we just couldn't get the town well to come back. And there's a whole bunch of stuff hanging around in the breeze that won't—we probably won't ever be able to reconstruct how much money is going to be spent in this town from October 10th, two, three years out.
>
> I know that the highway guys are thinking they're going to spend another twelve million bucks…We know we're going to spend fifty or sixty or seventy thousand dollars putting the Millot Green back together, and we know that we spent $700,000 on dirt roads, but I don't know anybody who has the whole picture, which is probably all right because the big picture might be really discouraging.

Yet even when the selectmen tally up all the town's expenses, a large portion of the loss may be left out of the picture—the personal loss. "In this society we don't get information like that from private families," Selectman Matt Saxon observed, "We don't share that kind of thing. Some people talk about it, some people don't talk about it at all." Then of course there are all the second-hand losses. Delvina Kearney struggled to stay in business in the weeks after the flood. Even Matt Saxton was affected financially. With five months of full-time flood work, his personal business suffered. Yet, he sees no point in dwelling on it, or even tallying losses. "I don't know if anyone is adding up what they lost like that. There's certainly no point to it. The main thing is to go forward."

As It Is

> So I missed the high water. I missed the flood. And so I have been in a place trying to understand what it all meant. I have spent the first few weeks just walking up and down the debris channel. I have eaten every meal down at the town hall with the Red Cross and the Salvation Army. It's one thing to intellectually understand what happened, but it is another thing entirely to try to understand what happened emotionally. And I am not sure if I get it. And as I get more distant from it, I am not sure if I ever will get it.
>
> *Matt Saxton*

Perhaps the flood cannot be understood. Even in the words of those who lost everything and those who tried to help them find it again, the experience is incomplete. And when those words have been gathered in brief interviews, the character of the voices ironed out into text, sorted, organized, narrated—more is lost, until by the time the story emerges it is only a glimpse of the event. "We could probably talk the rest of the afternoon," says Christopher Lyons of his own experience. Even if his story could be recorded and presented in full, it would be just a piece of a much greater event. So how could Matt Saxton, even with all his searching up and down the river, how could anyone who missed that wave, comprehend what even those who didn't miss the high waters, who didn't miss the flood, are still trying to understand? Like Matt, perhaps we can only be trying.

Why?

"Things happen for a reason. Someday we'll find out, someday we will," says Justin Canfield who lost his aunt and uncle to the flood. Yet it can be both hard to wait and hard to accept, and some are accustomed to neither. "I mean, we're Americans. Disasters happen elsewhere," says Anton Elbers.

"Things happen for a reason," Courtney Porter unwittingly echoes Justin, "and you don't always get an answer to that reason." Yet this does not stop people from looking for that answer, and several have been posited. "In general, I think people are believing this is a natural event," says Selectman Joel McCarty. Almut Yakovleff seems to be one of those. "I've always believed that nature has more power than we'd sometimes like to believe." Klaus Bayr agrees from the point of view of a geographer:

Seeing all of the town's people together was the most emotionally shattering of all.

~Brianna Smidutz (age 12)

If you look at the landscape, it's a narrow valley, and I think there was a very great possibility that something could have happened. Obviously it took a lot of water, a lot of rain to trigger this, but it's a narrow valley and narrow valleys are prone to have floods because where should all the water go?…It's a floodplain, a plain that needs to be flooded. The river puts it there in case too much water comes.

Some wondered about global warming being a contributing cause of the flood. Others see a human hand behind the wave, reaching out from varying distances in history. Joel McCarty speculated, "Perhaps [it] was magnified by manmade structures…Certainly there were no houses on that river a hundred twenty-five years ago, two hundred years ago, and a flood of that magnitude wouldn't have made any difference to anybody because they wouldn't have lost anything." Nearer to the present, Joel suggests another culprit."If we'd gone back to 1968 or so, we probably would have been smarter than to put that twelve-foot culvert at the end of that big swamp up by Cooper Hill, because without that manmade obstruction the flood still would have been dramatic and destructive…but we wouldn't have had that sudden surge of water." Or perhaps it was another lack of foresight. "If we had some kind of real emergency notification system like they do around the power plant in Vernon," Joel continued, "we might have been able to save some lives." One could also look to the erratic weather. "We are getting a lot of water. Winters aren't like they used to be," David Crosby observed.

Site of the culvert at Cooper Hill Road. Left: Fill supporting road overlies dark grey glacial till. Right: Former road surface was 55 feet above the eroded bed of Warren Brook. The base of the culvert was 47 feet below the road surface.
Photographs courtesy of the New Hampshire Geological Survey.

So, was it the fault of people who built their homes in the floodplain or of later builders who cut corners in construction; the fault of the builders of the culvert on Cooper Hill; the fault of the road agent for not, somehow, foreseeing the whole event; the fault of the police chief for not using force to get people out of their homes; the fault of someone or everyone in some way or other?

Asking "Why?" however, need not always imply fault. Perhaps the question could be placed in a different context. When Marlene Wade looked back on the loss of her home, she wondered why she had been spared. "I always have said that it's Divine intervention that I'm here, because if you had seen what had happened afterwards you would have wondered how we ever could escape." And David Crosby, as he watched the wave travel down the road, remembers, "It hit these ledges by the swimming hole. If those ledges hadn't been there to turn that water, it would have come down right through the center of Alstead and there would have been nothing left. Nothing."

States of Mind

"Some people were just amazing," Selectman Matt Saxton remembers, "how they took this in as a new fact and dealt with it. Other people sat down in the middle of the road and cried, waiting for somebody to save them. According to Joel McCarty, who fell into which category was almost predetermined:

Residents learn about forthcoming fluvial geomorphologic study, June 2006.
Photograph by David Moody

> *The flood was only there for a few hours, but the results will last a lifetime.*
>
> ~Chris French (age 12)

It's somewhat discouraging that events of great magnitude don't actually transform people. They tend to magnify them. So if you had sat me down with the voter list before the flood and said, "Just pretend we're going to have a big disaster next weekend. Who on this list do you predict will act like a hero and who will be a pain and a whiner?" I think in a small town we know each other a little too well, because I think my predictions would have been spot-on.

Paul Garatoni, whose house was severely damaged by the flood, has personally had enough of whining:

> Everyone's like, 'I don't want a loan: I've worked all my life…' What do you think my savings went into when we bought this? We shot the wad; we paid cash for it; that was our savings and since then…we had two thousand dollars in the bank…that's gone. How quick it can go!…I'm going to have a mortgage until I die; I know that.
> So big deal!…'Well, I don't want a mortgage, I'm fifty-six years old.' Well I'm sixty-two, Mister!…they complain about taxes…they want a full buy-out—who's going to pay for that? They want to sue—who's going to pay for that? Why not just say, "The hell with it!" go with it, do the best you can, and take good care of these people…They got a little town and we got whacked.

Paul and Maggie Garatoni's house being restored. *Photograph by Ken Walsh*

Most people have been doing just that—helping where they can and trying to be positive. As he was rebuilding roads, Craig Forest was amazed by the responses of the affected residents. "We did talk to quite a few of the victims while we were working out there. I was surprised at how positive an attitude they did have after what they went through." Rick Oberst was equally impressed. "I was amazed at how, looking at how destroyed the area was, people could cope with it." Matt Goodell, for one, didn't feel he had the right to be upset. "There were houses all around that were completely washed away. A good friend of mine lost his house. So it was kind of hard to feel bad about our losses." Yet the Goodells suffered no small loss. "We lost about sixty percent of all we owned…somewhere between fifteen and twenty thousand dollars worth of stuff."

Not only were they upbeat about their losses, but many residents came together to actively help those who were in greater need. "I can't say enough about them; it was awesome how they just banded together!" says Donna Olmstead. Comparing Alstead's response to the recent flooding in Louisiana, Betty Nash said, "It just seemed like Alstead pulled together better…Everybody pulled together from all different alleys. We just did what we had to do to help get back on our feet."

Hope for the future of Alstead. *Drawing by Rachel Therrien (age 9)*

> *The flood only lasted two days, but the memories will last forever.*
>
> ~Brian Blaisdell (age 12)

Marlene Wade felt the effects of such abundant generosity. "I love Alstead…it's really unimaginable that the people in a small community would come together so much…They had this [Christmas] program, The Giving Tree. This whole room was full of gifts."

Sharon Perry has stories of her own:

> I did want to tell you about some of my heroes, though. A couple of things that happened that week—I still can't believe it. We were at the fire station; it was Monday or Tuesday, and Tommy Canfield was there, and he was looking for his brother. And he came up to me and Ernie, and he said,
> "My camper's all set up. It's ready to stay in if you need a place to stay. You can stay in the camper any time."
> Good god! This man is looking for his brother—and you know his brother's dead—and he's offering us a place to stay! What kind of compassion is that? I couldn't believe it. I still can't believe it.
> And a couple of days later Kim Kercewich came up to me in the fire station and he said, "I'm really sorry. I wish I could have done more."
> And I said, "Kim, you did everything you could."
> But people were thinking about us. They did everything they could, [even though] they had losses much greater than mine. They were still reaching out to other people. I will never forget that, ever. That's why I'm going back to Alstead. The people are just too good.

Perhaps the good feelings will outlive the flood. "It just goes to show you," said David Crosby, "that when something like this happens, people really can work together. They don't have to fight and argue like they normally do in everyday life." The good wishes overcome more than just anger or resentment: they put an end to the apathy that builds up over the years. "So much goes on that we don't even realize, day to day," Lorraine Dustin observed. "We're so busy in our own activities, but something like this…you get a chance to pull together." Joel McCarty has lived here for thirty-five years, and he's met people in this project whom he's "never run into at the dump or the store or the church or the town office. Yet they've had the same experience. That's all pretty cool." And Matt Saxton feels the same: "The biggest, greatest good that came out of this is that we all know each other so much better. I know many more people than I used to, and that's true of everybody—everybody who was touched by this."

Alstead Today

Overleaf:
Tammy's Brick Shop Floral, located in the former Odd Fellows building, is open for business. *Photograph courtesy of The Alstead Historical Society*

In twenty-five years we may decide this was the best thing that ever happened to this town because it changed the landscape, and we had a chance to pull together as a community for a common purpose. But right now the wounds are pretty raw, and I don't think anyone sees a silver lining in this event. All they can see is the loss. I don't think that's unfair. I don't think that means they're incomplete human beings.

Joel McCarty

Despite so much effort to think positively and move forward, for many it is difficult to move on with the constant reminder of Alstead as it was juxtaposed with Alstead as it is. For many, driving down the same roads they have driven for years and seeing the ripped-up soil where their childhood homes used to sit, heightens the sense of loss. "All these years there have been homes there that you've just taken for granted, and now it's all gone," says Lorraine Dustin. Dale adds, "For us old-timers it's all quite surreal."

For many, the sense of security has also been lost. "I feel there's no protection," says Almut Yakovleff. "I mean, the house is basically on the river, and there's no trees so I feel very

Tent on Millot Green for Alstead's Flood Anniversary Reflection ceremonies, October 8-9, 2006. Cold River in foreground.
Photograph by David Moody

vulnerable to flooding—even spring flooding." Tom J. Hancock shares Almut's worries: "Home doesn't feel as secure," he says. Even rain has its effect on many residents. "The rain this last weekend, it worried me," remembers Kitty Kmiec. "I never used to think about going places in the rain, but now when it rains, it's like, *How many bridges do I have to cross to get where I'm going?"* For many residents, the sense of impending danger may take years to dispel.

To some extent the initial shock has faded. "We're past the point of reeling, trying to regroup and get our footing," says Kitty, "but we're not to the security spot again. We're just waiting out the winter…Once spring comes, we'll start rebuilding and trying to figure out where we are." Almut has repaired her foundations: "The wall has been put back up, and the home is good and snug and tight for winter." Yet for those like Almut, even a returned sense of security feels temporary, and many were waiting to see what the new year would bring. "It's hard to be patient when you live by the river," she said. "You look at the whole picture and you think ahead to spring and summer." Perhaps the full extent of the damage won't be understood until residents can compare the spring-time river—stripped of its trees and plants, its large boulders and old swimming holes—with the river of their memories.

The newly restored baseball field on Millot Green. *Photograph by David Moody*

For some, even the memories are slipping away. "It's kind of weird," Courtney Porter admits, "because I catch myself looking around, and thinking, *Why can't I remember what it looked like?* I don't know why my brain's looking at it now the way that it is…When you look at the same thing over and over again, you kind of take it for granted; when it changes drastically, you're like, *Huh?*"

On the bright side, some long-lost memories have been discovered. Before the Millot Green was rebuilt, the Alstead Historical Society worked cooperatively with Vilas Middle School students to search Millot Green for artifacts from Alstead's earlier days. Among their findings are buttons and buckles from the eighteenth and ninteenth centuries and antique pottery shards. Kitty Kmiec found pieces of her own family history that had been stashed away by her grandmother—old letters, one dating back to 1772, the other to 1838, and "a lot of things that had been in the family for a while, but we hadn't realized that we had until we started going through things." Rick Oberst, meanwhile, was learning the history of the town as he worked repairing roads:

> Trying to put things back together, people would have recollections of years ago…There were some interesting stories going around. A lot of history was coming out…I think it was good for everyone to have that opportunity [to

Artifacts recovered from Millot Green. *Photograph courtesy of The Alstead Historical Society*

146

talk]. A lot of the locals would come out while we were working to share stories about forty, fifty years ago—who lived where and what businesses were around. It was an education…I'd never known there was a series of mills along the river.

Today, there seems to be a general consensus that those involved in rebuilding Alstead are remarkable.

> Joel and Matt have done an outstanding job. Chris Lyons, Bob Bromley—everyone who's had to deal with this—who's never signed up for anything like this—has done an outstanding job. The fire department, all the local volunteers, everybody…even Governor Lynch when he came… DOT, Whitcomb Construction, Eastern Logging—all the subcontractors were so devoted. They were working seven days a week, eight-weeks-plus, nonstop. Their dedication to this town was just incredible."
>
> *Delvina Kearney*

Tammy Gendron wrote, "Our highway crew, fire department, and police force, were nothing short of miraculous, and I certainly believe they deserve every accolade given."

In April, Selectman Joel McCarty summarized the progress in Alstead:

> There's no manual that came with the flood to tell us what we were supposed to be doing, and we're sort of stumbling along and figuring our way out of it. I think the key difference that people lose sight of is that the roads and bridges and telephone poles and electric lines…have been pretty well put back together. In fact, some of them are actually better after the flood than [they were] before.
>
> But the federal programs that we administered were actually pretty weak when it comes to providing assistance for individual families. So really just about all we've been doing for the last three and a half to four months is trying to find programs for relief and material and diesel fuel and furnaces and fuse boxes and dirt…for private households that weren't protected by insurance or broader federal programs. So we've just become explorers on an alien landscape.
>
> We've certainly had some successes, but I think we're a lot closer to the beginning than we are to the end. I think, for instance, we're sneaking up on six months from the flood…and we have a minimum of two more years of flood work to do. We're trying to build some houses across the river to relocate flood families to, and I can't imagine that any one of these

---

The Millot Green, the place everybody in Alstead used, lost everything, even color.

~ Mallory Fredriksen (age 11)

> *It was all right because the flood went away.*
>
> ~ Katie Nelson
> (age 3)

houses will be occupied before the fall. I'll be very, very pleased if we could get people in those on the anniversary date of the flood. There's so much paper and so many meetings, and a lot of obstacles that I don't think we're anywhere near where we need to be.

Since April some wonderful progress has been made—mainly the passing of the "Buy-out" legislation in Concord. The bill, approved almost unanimously by the New Hampshire General Court, will buy demolished properties at their assessed value before the flood, minus any aid owners have received from FEMA or other sources. A committee of state and local leaders will convene to determine what will be done with the land. The passing of the "Buy-out" bill strengthened the townspeople's hope. As customers drift in and out of her general store, Delvina Kearney has been watching the transformation:

> If you think back, we're all in mourning right now. I call it mourning because we've lost a part of Alstead, we've lost roads, we've lost houses, we've lost people—but yet people have a lot left because they have each other. And if you have your life, you can always start all over again. That's probably sometimes hard, but there's hope.
>
> When people come in the store it's great. I mean there are good comments now—not sad ones. People's faces are cheerier–it's not the sullen look all the time. You can actually see hope that things are really going to do quite well.

The Future

"Come back next year, the 9th of October," Paul Garatoni says, "and you are going to see one of the biggest parties going, because we rebuilt…You gotta celebrate, because you turn on the TV at night and look around at what Hurricane Katrina did. Then, even if you're wiped out with nothin'…then you see: my little town was spared that."

Although there is real reason to rejoice over Alstead's reconstruction, for some, like Bill Seale's widow, Linda Anderson, the future holds too many grim reminders of the past.

> The Farmers' Market opens, usually the first weekend in May, and that was a big part of our life…it was an intense time of year for us, and a good time of year…[Bill] enjoyed the people at the Farmers' Market and he would do special things for people.
>
> It's going to be totally different. It was his livelihood while [for] other

people…this was just a weekend hobby kind of thing. He was there in snow, sleet, rain, whatever. He didn't stay home because it was bad weather. He was out there doing the job. It just meant the world to him.

Linda is not the only one who is ambivalent about the future. "Some families are still having trouble," Mary Lou Huffling noted. "We're averaging sixty-five to seventy families at the Food Shelf still. This is twice the usual number."

"This is by far the biggest event that Alstead ever had, at least in my lifetime," Dale Dustin stated. "I hope it's the last." Most people seem to think it will be. "I don't think it could ever happen again," says Kitty Kmiec. "They talk about a hundred-year storm. I think this is the once-in-the-course-of-history storm." The flood widened the channel, making another flood seem unlikely. David Crosby agrees: "They are saying it's a five-hundred-year flood—and in five hundred years, I'm not going to worry about it…But I notice, from Lake Warren down through, there's nothing there to hold the water back anymore, no obstruction in the brook." Yet David wants to be safe. "I don't want to ever put a culvert back in Cooper Hill: I want to leave that a dead-end road." When this was announced at the town meeting after the flood, the crowd let out a big round of applause.

Banners on timberframe "bandstand" on Millot Green. *Photograph courtesy of The Alstead Historical Society*

> *The only thing you can learn from this is to appreciate what you have, for it could all be gone after a simple rainfall.*
>
> *~ Sarah DeValk (age 11)*

> *Next time people get a call saying there is a flood, we will probably pay more attention to it.*
>
> *~ Tyler Gendron (age 11)*

The flood is a lesson for all those in similar situations. "It's a huge ripple effect," says Jim Fowle, "and hopefully it's rippling more than we even know because hopefully other people in other towns have seen what happened here and can work not to allow it to happen there." Klaus Bayr suggests some alternatives that would be helpful for communities wishing to avoid such a disaster:

> If this were to happen again…Either they build a dam there so the water would be released in a controlled fashion, or move the houses out of the floodplain…It teaches us that people should be wise where they put their houses and where to construct things.

The lessons may be appropriate for future Alstead residents as well. "I can't imagine anyone in the near future rebuilding any of these areas," said Dale Dustin. "I wouldn't. That doesn't mean that someone else wouldn't, over time." When the memory of the flood has faded and the river is once more a narrow waterway sheltered by trees, who might forget? The same is true of another lesson, according to David Crosby, a lesson that some Alstead residents learned the hard way: "The only thing I can guarantee, is that the next time we come knocking on their doors and tell them to leave, they will leave—until the next generation comes, and they don't know about it."

For the near future, however, Alstead's residents are left with their hopes. Kitty Kmiec would like to see growth—in both the landscape and the community.

> It would be nice if some of those places could be turned into parks and places that people can use, but I just don't know. There's still so much more negotiating that needs to go on to figure out where to go from here. I'd like to think that [the flood has] pulled the townspeople together, that we'll be stronger, but I've heard that it may not be that way, that many people are still angry about what happened. It's a disaster. It's something that nobody wanted to happen, but it did and I think we all just need to pick ourselves up out of the mud and go on.

Like Kitty's wishes, most hopes for the town are modest, rooted in the town as a whole or in the natural landscape that was—and must still be—home. "I would very much like to have the river put back," says Almut Yakovleff, "and have the channel maintained and some sense of security for all of us living along the river." Jokingly she adds, "I mean if they want to build a ten-foot stone wall, that would be fine with me too. I could plant roses on top of the wall, and pretend I'm at the ocean." Linda Anderson, meanwhile, has a simple wish. "We have one tree on our property which is standing…I will try really hard to get them not to cut that tree down."

Many share the hope of rebuilding Millot Green, now "Millot Brown" according to several sixth-graders. In her store across from Millot Green, it was hard for Delvina Kearney to watch its transformation from a green park to a pile of debris. "The most horrific part was when they used Millot Green as their salvage area, and the cars were piling up…It was nice to see the cleanup. It was devastating, but as it got cleaned up, it gave you a sense of, 'It's going to get back to normal.'"

Alstead Municipal office building, October 2006. *Photograph courtesy of The Alstead Historical Society*

> *If something like this happens again, will we be ready?*
>
> ~ Jamie MacDonald (age 12)

In an interview in March, David Crosby described the status of the green: "The selectmen gave it to me and said, 'Do what's got to be done.'" After surveys had been completed, he turned the project over to Clarence Myers, who is currently in the process of reconstructing the green as it had been. High school senior Matt Barnes looks forward to the reconstruction:

> I plan on living in this same area when I grow up with a wife and family. I want my kids to be able to have the same type of place I did. I want to be able to watch them play sports down at the Millot Green when they are small. I also want them to be able to go down there with their friends when they are old enough. Because of the flood, it won't look the same or even be the same place, but hopefully it will be rebuilt so that my kids can grow up and have their own memories.

With the Millot soon rebuilt, the roads repaired, and families resettling, Alstead should be almost back to normal in a few years, but those who have lived here longest know things can never be the same. "Alstead will be different from now on," says Shelley Barnes, "Although they've made remarkable progress, Alstead is definitely different…It's not the same feeling." Lorraine Dustin reflects:

> Newcomers to the town won't know what the town looked like before, and it will probably have no effect on them. But anyone who knows Alstead, when they come into the town, it will probably be devastating to them. It's so barren. Houses have been washed away and they look like kindling.… The people who were in our classes at school…when they come back to see it, I just can't imagine what it's going to do to them.

Perhaps if people had seen the state of Alstead on October 9, 2005, if they had traveled down the river, watching wires snapping, trees crashing, and then if they had seen the days that followed, the aid pouring in, neighbors helping neighbors shovel mud from their living rooms…if they could have seen all of this and then compared it to Alstead as it is, perhaps they would understand why Maggie Gacek could say with such confidence, "Alstead won't be the Alstead of my childhood, but it will survive."

Epilogue

...And Always The Waters

It was a thick jungle going from our house to the river; now it is an empty desert.

Almut Yakovleff

And now, since the flood, all we have is a big ravine with no trees and no features left.

Bruce Bellows

It ain't never gonna be the same. It ain't never gonna be the same. The river has changed for good.

Erwin Ward

All these frogs were deep in their hibernation grounds along Warren Brook by October 8, 2005, and the force of the flood scooped them all up and washed them away with everything else. The spring of 2006 was silent; I struggled to hear a few lone peepers and one grey tree frog.

Carol Drummond

Outback was almost like a wildlife sanctuary for us. We had Baltimore orioles, cardinals, goldfinches; it was a bird's paradise…so that's all gone and that's hard. You know, I miss the birds' song; there's no birds' songs. Occasionally I'll see one blue jay—looking for something.

Almut Yakovleff

The new river is too new; we will need many years of autumn leaves and spring swallows to soften its lines.

Lark Leonard

The day after the 2005 flood, we walked over some of the broken pieces of pavement near the mill. In one of the great cracks between them, we spotted a bit of bedrock, and someone remarked, "That rock is the reason we are here."

Margaret Chase Perry

Overleaf:
Cold River near the confluence of Warren Brook.
Photograph by Mike Heidorn

Our community has changed in many ways: the river, roads, houses, and some of the people. But one thing that will never change in our community is the love and caring that we all show one another.

Lisa Brehio

Thanksgiving Day, and we sat here and ate dinner, and looked out there and it was all snow-covered; it was beautiful, because of course you couldn't see all the brown dirt, and there was a brown heron out there—we'd never seen one before—just kind of poking around in the water. It was like this little gift.

Mary Larsen

Warren Brook below Lake Warren Dam, East Alstead. *Photograph courtesy of Tafi Brown*

Looking upstream on the Cold River behind the Newell Mill (partly seen on the right). Charlie Brady lives next to the red summer house which was built on the former millrace of Newell Mill. *Photograph by Heather Gendron*

Cold River Song
Charlie Brady

Friday morning it began to rain,
Weatherman said tomorrow'd be the same
Saturday came, it poured and poured,
Cold River just rose more and more

All thru the day they watched the water rise
Folks on Lake Warren couldn't believe their eyes
Water rolling on down past Chase's Mill,
Down 123 to the base of the hill

Saturday night the rain still came down,
Creeks started washing over streets in town
The river's too rough, the river's too wide,
Won't get much sleep tonight

Under the gray October skies,
The water in the hollow began to rise
Ain't nowhere for the water to go,
People settled in the valley below

They feared the dam couldn't hold much more,
So police started going from door to door
"Get out now while you still can"
Some folks stayed, some folks ran

Sunday the word came down from Cooper Hill Road,
The culvert below the hollow, man, it just let go
There's a wall of water heading down your way,
Ain't nothing to do now but hope and pray

Folks below started hearing a sound,
Trees began to fall and wires came down
Someone on the shore they let out a cry as they
Saw their neighbor's house floating by

Cars and trucks swept over the bridges in town,
Garages and barns ripped right out of the ground,
Just like an arrow shot straight thru the heart.
The river tore this town apart

Charlie Brady *is a songwriter who lives in Alstead. His house overlooks the Cold River. Charlie regularly performs his work at clubs in Southern New Hampshire.*

Appendix A

How Bad Was the Flood?

Over the years Alstead has had many floods of varying degree. The town's annual reports are full of descriptions by the Board of Selectmen and the Road Agent of damages to the roads, bridges, and culverts caused by floods. Yet this event was different.

Shortly after the October 2005 flood, the New Hampshire-Vermont Water Science Center of the U.S. Geological Survey (USGS), in Pembroke, N.H., surveyed high water marks of the flood. With funds from the Federal Emergency Management Agency, the USGS conducted a study of the depth of flooding, the peak discharges, and the flood-flow frequency characteristics of the flood. The following information is abstracted from their report.[32]

Warren Brook at Mill Hollow. The USGS estimates that the peak discharge of the flood where Warren Brook crosses Forest Road was 820 cubic feet per second (cfs) and 7 to 11 ft above the channel of the brook. The recurrence interval of a flow of this magnitude is greater than 100 years.

Warren Brook at Cooper Hill Road. The Cooper Hill road embankment at the peak of the flood around 6:00 a.m. on Sunday morning impounded a lake of about 42 acres containing 421 acre-feet.* When the embankment was breached, the contents of the lake rushed downstream. The magnitude of the peak discharge depends upon the rate at which the embankment failed. Using a dam-break model, the USGS estimated that the peak discharge immediately downstream of the culvert on Warren Brook was 24,900 cfs and 20,100 cfs at the confluence with the Cold River. The maximum flood elevations downstream of Cooper Hill Road ranged from 15-20 ft above the channel bed consistent with eyewitness accounts of a "wall of water" 15-20 ft high. At the mouth of Warren Brook the high water mark was at an elevation 25 ft above the channel bed and 15 ft above the Acworth Road Bridge (Route123A) across Warren Brook. The peak flow experienced downstream of Cooper Hill Road was in the order of 2.6 times the average daily discharge (9,380 cfs) of the Connecticut River at North Walpole, N.H.

Cold River at Vilas Pool Dam. At Vilas Pool, a large percentage of the flow was diverted down Acworth Road from the pool. The estimate peak discharge for the storm was 6,370 cfs. At the peak, the water level was about 9 feet above the crest of the dam and about 14 ft above the channel bed just upstream of the confluence of Warren Brook. This peak discharge has a recurrence interval of about 100 years.

*An acre-foot is the amount of water that covers one acre to a depth of one foot

Cold River at Alstead Village Bridge. The Cold River at the Alstead Village Bridge had a high water elevation about 26 ft above the river channel and about 3 ft above the road bed of the bridge.

Cold River at Drewsville Gorge. Peak discharge at the Drewsville bridge was estimated to be 21,800 cfs. The high water level was about 23.7 ft above the streambed. The recurrence interval of flow of this magnitude is greater than 500 years. The previous maximum discharge for the river at Drewsville for the period 1940 to 1978 was 6,710 cfs in December 1973. The peak stage for October 9, 2005, was 11.4 ft higher than the December 1973 flood.

The Flood in Retrospect

The extreme rainfall over the steep slopes, shallow impermeable soils, and narrow valleys of the Cold River watershed combined with the failure of the Cooper Hill Road culvert to create the devastating flood. Given the eyewitness accounts of the very large vortex that formed at the inlet to the Cooper Hill Road culvert and of the jet of water discharging from the culvert outlet, it is highly unlikely that the culvert was obstructed. It simply could not discharge a large enough volume of water to offset the inflow of water to Spooner Flats.

The description of the level of the water impounded by the Cooper Hill Road culvert surging upwards in pulses by those monitoring the site, suggests that the flow into Spooner Flats was not uniform. One possible cause of the surges was the successive collapse of small beaver dams breached by the high runoff in the Camp Brook watershed and other small watersheds in the drainage basin upstream from the culvert.

Once breached, Warren Brook carved a gorge approximately 110 ft wide and 55 ft deep and eroded the bed of the brook 8 ft below the base of the former culvert in a highly compacted glacial till described as having the density of concrete.[33] The culvert pipe was washed out and transported 0.6 mi downstream. The size of the boulders and cobbles transported by the flood wave, the crushing of vehicles of all types and their transport miles downstream, and the total destruction of homes and buildings along the Warren Brook and the Cold River all bear testimony to the awesome power of water.

By any measure, the Alstead Flood of October 2005 was an extraordinary event.

Appendix B

The Flood Chronology*

Saturday, October 8

4:00 P.M.   Cumulative rainfall at East Alstead is 3.40 inches.

7:07 P.M.   Water reported running over Pine Cliff Road in front of Lake Warren dam. Water on the road flows over the hard top road on to Forest Road (Rt. 123) and down Hatch Hill eroding drainage ditches on both sides of the road. A 6-ft culvert over halfway down the hill filled with gravel washed from the ditches and probably was soon overcome by the volume of water coming down Warren Brook and Forest Road. David Crosby reported water running down the state road in front of the Town Barn because the 10-ft wide, 70-ft long, multiplate pipe arch that carries Warren Brook from south to north under Forest Road at the foot of Hatch Hill had plugged up. Kim Kercewich reports that "Water is all over East Alstead."

9:00 P.M.   Water at Vilas Pool observed running over the concrete sidewalk by David Crosby and Kim Kercewich. Tom Marron reports the road flooding on Forest Road at the foot of Hatch Hill by the 10-ft. wide culvert.

10:00 P.M. Emergency personnel told to report to the East Alstead and Alstead Village Fire Stations to assist. People begin to evacuate from houses between the foot of Hatch Hill and the Town Barn. Spooner Flats started to fill with water.

10:30 P.M. The sides of Forest Road at the Town Barn start washing out. At the top of Hatch Hill, a foot or so of water is washing down the road and undermining sections of asphalt. Warren Brook cuts a channel through Forest Road about 40 feet west of the culvert in front of the Marron place.

Inlet to 12-ft Cooper Hill Road culvert covered with water. Inflow of water from Warren Brook and Camp Brook to Spooner Flats is larger than the discharge capacity of the culvert. The water level in Spooner Flat upstream of the culvert rapidly rises.

11:00 P.M. The 100-year recurrence interval, 24-hour rainfall amount of 6.10 inches is exceeded in East Alstead. A total of 6.49 inches had fallen since the storm began. Crews close Forest Road at Cooper Hill Road. A vortex forms over the submerged culvert inlet. Fire Chief Kercewich and Police Chief Lyons decide to evacuate residents on Warren Brook in the Cooper Hill Road area.

*Data are from the logs of Keene Mutual Aid and the Alstead Emergency Operations Center. Meterological and hydrological data are from the sources cited in chapter 1.

11:45 P.M.　　Selectmen notified of precautionary evacuations. An emergency communications center is set up at Police Headquarters in the basement of the Town Municipal Building on Mechanic Street. Fire Chief Kercewich moves to Alstead Village to coordinate the evacuations from there.

12:00 P.M.　　Cumulative rainfall for the preceding 24-hour period reaches 7.37 inches for East Alstead, 1.2 times the magnitude of the 100-year, 24-hour storm. The water level at the Cooper Hill Road culvert is 5 to 6 feet over the top of the culvert inlet.

Sunday, October 9

12:15 A.M.　　David Crosby leaves the Town Barn for the last time and drives through Spooner Flats in water up to the lettering on the side of his town truck door.

1:00 A.M.　　According to John Mann, a resident of Mill Hollow, the water in Lake Warren exceeded the maximum height of the dam's spillway and water was running over the earthen/stone parts of the dam.[35] The dam ordinarily would release about 450 cfs (cubic feet per second) with water at the top of the dam spillway.

1:14 A.M.　　Chief Kercewich activates the Lake Warren Dam Emergency Plan. Chief Lyons advises Keene Mutual Aid dispatcher that Lake Warren dam is at Code Yellow and that evacuations of homes along Forest Road are in progress.

1:20 A.M.　　NH Hampshire Office of Emergency Management is notified of the action.

2:35 A.M.　　Police Lt. Bromley advises dispatcher that residents along Forest Road from Cooper Hill Road to Alstead Center Road (Route 12A) are being asked to evacuate. Some are refusing to leave.

3:00 A.M.　　Water level temporarily stabilizes at the Cooper Hill Road culvert.

4:31 A.M.　　Emergency personnel at the East Alstead Fire Station report that the south side of the Lake Warren Dam is eroding. They are monitoring the dam.

5:30 A.M.　　No change in the condition of Lake Warren dam. Water level behind Cooper Hill Road culvert is within 2 ft of the road surface. The water is 33 ft over the top of the culvert inlet.

5:56 A.M.　　Sunrise on Sunday, October 9.

6:07 A.M.　　Water level at Lake Warren dam is reported to be dropping. Cumulative rainfall of the storm in East Alstead as of 6:00 a.m. was 10.13 inches. Rainfall during the 6 hours between midnight and 6 a.m. was 2.63 inches.

6:08 A.M.　　Water running over Cooper Hill Road. At this point the water impounded on Spooner Flats amounted to 421 acre-feet. The downstream side of the embankment of the road was armored with riprap stone, which helped protect the embankment from erosion. However, water flowing down the northeast side of Forest Road (the opposite side of the road from the impounded brook) was diverted by a rise in the road westward across the pavement and started to erode the downstream corner where Cooper Hill Road and Forest Road intersect. The resulting erosion begins to undermined the protective layer of riprap.

6:10 A.M.　　Code Red declared for Cooper Hill culvert along the Cold River. Evacuation called for River Street and all areas downstream of the culvert.

6:15 A.M.　　Code Red declared for Lake Warren Dam.

6:40 A.M.　　David Crosby leaves Cooper Hill to assist with the evacuation on River Street.

6:55 A.M.　　Keene Mutual Aid is asked to alert Langdon and Walpole to the possibility of a sudden surge in the Cold River.

6:57 A.M.　　National Grid [power utility] log reports power interrupted in Alstead.

7:01 A.M.　　Cooper Hill culvert "let loose." As the water running off Forest Road undermines the riprap, pieces fall into the growing cut allowing the water overtopping Cooper Hill Road to start washing away the embankment that in turn caused the roadway to collapse. This in turn allowed more water to pour through the rapidly growing gap in the embankment which both widened and cut downward toward the culvert pipe. This process of embankment failure was not instaneous and appears to have taken place in several stages. The first breeching caused a sudden release of water from Spooner Flats that caused a surge or small flood wave that traveled downstream.

7:10 A.M.　　Matt Saxton's mother, while talking to her son on the telephone from her home on Cobb Hill Road reports, "I am watching the bottom of Cooper Hill wash away." This released a large flood wave–the "wall of water" that devastated Alstead. The collapse of the Cooper Hill Road embankment appears to have taken at least 20 minutes and possibly longer.[36]

7:19 A.M.　　The town lost electric power.

7.23 A.M.　　Michelle Koson and Kim Kercewich evacuate the command center in the police station by breaking down the door to the selectmen's offices upstairs to escape the rapidly rising water on Millot Green. The time is recorded by a signal sent by an "intrusion" alarm in the office.

7:25 A.M.　　"All hell broke loose" in Alstead Village.

Endnotes

1. Frink, Helen, *Alstead Through the Years.* (Alstead, NH: Alstead Historical Society, 1992), p. 2-5.
2. *Ibid.*, p. 98
3. Chase, Heman, *Short History of Mill Hollow* (Springfield, VT: Edmund and Mary Hurd, 1969), p. 3.
4. Frink, *Alstead Through the Years,* p. 100.
5. Frink, *Alstead Through the Years,* p. 122-123.
6. Frink, *Alstead Through the Years,* p. 461.
7. See the Cold River Local Advisory Committee web site: http://www.coldriver.org
8. Zankel, Mark, *A Land Conservation Plan for the Ashuelot River Watershed* (Concord, NH: The Nature Conservancy, 2004).
9. River distances from Olson, Scott A., *Flood of October 8 and 9 on the Cold River in Walpole, Langdon, and Alstead and on Warren Brook in Alstead, New Hampshire* (US Geological Survey, 2006), Open-File Report 1221. Stream slopes were calculated from the same source.
10. Guinn, Dale F., *Emergency Inspection of Warren Lake Dam #005.04* (NH Department of Environmental Services, Dam Bureau), Inspection Report: 6 January 2006.
11. Burroughs, John. Telephone interviews with Lark Leonard, 23 and 27 July 2006.
12. *Alstead Annual Town Report 1967,* p. 13.
13. *Alstead Annual Town Report 1968,* p. 45.
14. *Alstead Annual Town Report 1969,* p. 13.
15. *Alstead Annual Town Report 1971,* p. 12.
16. *Alstead Annual Town Report 1991,* p. 18.
17. John C. Ridge, Tufts University, Department of Geology, has mapped these glacial deposits in great detail. See Ridge, John C., *Surficial Geologic Map of the Walpole and Gilsum 7.5-Minute Quadrangles, New Hampshire-Vermont* (NH Geological Survey, COGEOMAP 1990, Geo-157) and *Surficial Geologic Map of the Alstead 7.5-Minute Quadrangle and Bellows Falls 7.5-Minute Quadrangle, Vermont-New Hampshire* (NH Geological Survey, STATEMAP 1998, Geo-167).
18. LeCompte, Douglas, "The United States Weather Highlights of 2005: A Stormy Year" *Weather Wise,* v. 59, no. 2 (2006), p. 30-37.
19. Belk, Nicole M., *Monthly Report of River/Flood Conditions* (Taunton, MA: National Oceanographic and Atmospheric Administration, National Weather Service, 2 December 2005.
20. David Moody, Personal Communication, 20 July 2006.
21. Compiled by Michael Heidorn, Personal Communication, 20 December 2005.
22. Knox, C. E. and Nordenson, T. J. "Average Annual Runoff and Precipitation in the New England-New York Area" (U.S. Geological Survey, 1955), *Hydrologic Investigations Atlas HA-7.*
23. Cooper, Anderson, "360 Degrees" Cable News Network. Aired October 12, 2005, 19:00 EST.
24. Lane, Richard, "Geologic Hazard—New Hampshire Flood 2005" Granite State Geologist, v. 51. December, 2005.
25. Miller, Rebecca, "Lynch Signs Flood Relief Bill" *Claremont (NH) Eagle Times,* 8 June 2006.
26. Miller, "Flooding Hammers Region" *Claremont (NH) Eagle Times,* 10 October 2005.
27. Davis, Mark, "Lynch Estimates Flood Damage in Tens of Millions" *(NH) Valley News,* 13 October 2005.
28. Seitz, Stephen, "Lynch Focuses on Providing Tools to Aid Recovery" *New Hampshire Union Leader,* 15 October 2005.
29. Seitz, "Lynch Surveys Flood Relief Progress" *New Hampshire Union Leader,* 19 October 2005.
30. Seitz, "Towns Assess Damage" *New Hampshire Union Leader,* 11 October 2005.
31. Seitz, "Lynch Surveys Flood Relief Progress" *New Hampshire Union Leader,* 19 October 2005.
32. Olson, *Flood of October 8 and 9 on the Cold River.*
33. Lane, "Geologic Hazard—New Hampshire Flood 2005"
34. John Mann wrote an account of his experience of the flood and kindly shared it with the Alstead Historical Society.
35. Guinn, *Emergency Inspection of Warren Lake Dam #005.04*, p. 1.
36. Olson, *Flood of October 8 and 9 on the Cold River.*

Contributors

Many people gave generously of their time, photographs, and artwork to help the Alstead Historical Society and the schools "Save Our History." We are most grateful to all.

Fall Mountain Regional High School

The following students at Fall Mountain Regional High school, under the direction of teachers Taunya Lincoln (English) and William Ranauro (History), conducted and/or transcribed interviews about people's experiences of the Alstead flood.

Patrick Brewer	Anthony Goodhue	Karri Makinen	Michael Sellarole
Jay Chamberlin	James Healy	Emily Malnati	Alison Stoddard-Gruber
Abigail Collinsworth	Christopher Johnson	Kathleen Markiewicz	Charles Street
Emily Comstock	Nicholas Kranowski	Jacob McDougle	Colin Tatro
Jennifer Davey	Cassandra Kreek	Lindsey McGill	Tyler Tobin
Bryan Doyle	Olivia Lincoln	Megan McPherson	Brianna Tottenhoff
Maia Earl	Zachary Lincoln	Nicholas Parrott	Nicole Varone
Fay "Ellie" Richardson	Alison Livengood	Nicole Piccirillo	Rebecca Vogel
Erin Farrell	Elizabeth Livengood	Victor Punt	Stefanie Welling
Justin Foreman	Allisia MacDonald	Emily Ranauro	Kristina Zurmuhlen
Emilie Forstrom	Kaitlyn Mack	Ian Relihan	

Adults Interviewed

The people listed below kindly consented to being interviewed, sometimes more than once, about their experiences before, during, and after the Alstead flood.

Pamela Allen	Candy Fowle	Mary Larsen	Sharon Perry
Linda Anderson	James Fowle	Robert Larsen	Karen Plaisted
Matthew Barnes	Melissa Fredricksen	Lark Leonard	Cory Plummer
Michelle Barnes	Hazel Fuller	Olivia Lincoln	Courtney Porter
Klaus Bayr	John Fuller	Taunya Lincoln	Cameron Pryor
Bruce Bellows	Margaret Gacek	Zachary Lincoln	Darrah Ramsey
Gail Bellows	Paul Garatoni	Tina Lyman	Randy Rhoades
Alexandra Bley-Vroman	Tammy Gendron	Christopher Lyons	Matthew Saxton
Lisa Brehio	Matthew Goodell	Don Martin	Derek Sherburne
John Burroughs	Thomas J. Hancock	Joel McCarty	Jesse Sherburne
Justin Canfield	Thomas W. Hancock	Jacob McDougle	Julius Speaker
Craig Carmody	Daniel Higgins	Mary Ann Melquist	Ted Speaker
Martha Cooper	Mary H…	Henry Montcrief	Sherry Stanley
David Crosby	Meredith Howard	Jeanne Moody	Brandi Stetson
Jennifer Davey	Jan Howe	Betty Nash	Frances Thibault
Eliza Davis	Mary Lou Huffling	Diana Nelson	George Thompson
Carol Drummond	Joshua Ioannou	Ben Northcott	Karlene Thompson
Dale Dustin	Jolene Jones	Rick Oberst	Jean Vaillancourt
Lorraine Dustin	Delvina Kearney	David Olmstead	Joshua Wade
Anton Elbers	Kate Kelly	Donna Olmstead	Marlene Wade
Dove Elbers	Kim Kercewich	Christine Parrott	Erwin Ward
Eleanor Elbers	Bradley Kmiec	Nicolas Parrott	Wendy Ward
Tom Ferenc	Kitty Kmiec	Grace Perry	Barbara "Bobbie" Wilson
Craig Forrest	Randy Kmiec	Margaret Chase Perry	Almut Yakovleff

Children (Ages 3 through 12)

Children from The Orchard School, Alstead Primary School, and The Acworth School took part in interviews, drew pictures, and/or wrote stories about the flood.

Nikita Allen	Colleen Heidorn	Lauraann Marron	Jordan Plaisted
Dakota Barnes	Angela Hilow	Dylan Martin	Andrea Porter
Tasjia Barnes	Aidan Jasmin	Heidi Miller	Cade Porter
Emma Berg	Zev Kazati-Morgan	Katie Nelson	Hannah Rhoades
Christina Corona	Alexandra Kercewich	Luke H. Nelson	Peter Rhoades
Toben Fay	Ben Kercewich	Devin Olmstead	Sophia Rose
Kristy Fish	Lily Kitcher-MacNeil	Erica Page	Rachel Therrien
Clay Gendron	Renee LeBlanc	Nicole Page	Austin Wilson
Raymond Gosetti	Maddie Lord	Dylan Plaisted	Faith Wilson

Vilas Middle School

When the Vilas Middle School reopened on October 17, the sixth-grade students taught by Linda Ferland and Gerald Pavao wrote essays about their experiences of the flood. Some of their words were quoted in this book, and all the essays provided documentation for the project.

Logan Adams	Mallory Fredriksen	Meghan Hilow	Jacadi Simard
Jeremy Barnett	Chris French	Mary Locke	Marie Simoneaux
Brian Blaisdell	Micaela Gabardi	Jamie MacDonald	Brianna Smidutz
Alexis Burns	Zachary Garrow	Cassidy Morse	Jered Smith
Jarid Crosby	Daniel Gendron	Paige O'Dette	Sabrina Sodders
Elizabeth Cubberley	Mollie Gendron	Kevin Plummer	Joshua Sullivan
Sara DeValk	Tyler Gendron	Lauren Ramsey	Daniel Ziolkowski
Lyle Doolittle	Bradley Gordon	Grace Rushing	

Millot Green Artifact Recovery Project

Gregory Sherwood and David Germain, metal detectionists, led the effort to retrieve long-buried artifacts from Millot Green while the surface was still uncovered. Teacher Sharon Rabe coordinated the project with students from Vilas Middle School.

Holly Bengston	Carmen del Genio	Michael Knicely	Zackary Whittaker
Ashley Chase	Sonia Gosetti	Alex Waters	

Alstead Historical Society

Members of the Alstead Historical Society researched, collected and organized the data, documents and photographs used in writing this book. They also provided editorial guidance and coordinated the Save Our History project with the schools.

Bruce Bellows	Lorraine Dustin	Cindy Hendrick	Diana Nelson
Judy Bellows	C. David French	Heidi Hernes	Paul Rodrigue
Charles Brady	Heather Gendron	John Leonard	Gloria Seddon
Tafi Brown	David Germain	Lark Leonard	Gregory B. Sherwood
Carol Drummond	Erin Heidorn	David W. Moody	Howard Weeks
Dale Dustin	Michael Heidorn	Jeanne C. Moody	

News Media

The following news organizations donated courtesy copies of their photographs, videotapes, and/or interview transcripts for use in this book as well as in the Alstead Historical Society museum exhibit and archives.

Cable News Network (CNN)
Disaster News Network (DNN)
The Eagle Times (Claremont)
The Keene Sentinel

The River Record (Keene)
The New Hampshire Union Leader (Manchester)
The Weather Channel
WMUR-TV (Manchester)

Photographs

The Alstead Historical Society received over 7600 photographs, videotapes, and digital images of the flood and permissions to use them in this book. Some of the CDs with digital images contained works by more than one photographer, including some downloaded from the Internet. Photographs by one person were sometimes duplicated on disks submitted by several people. We have made every effort to track down the names of all those who actually took the pictures from which those in the book were selected. Some may be incorrect or remain unidentified, however.

Betsy Anderson
Linda Anderson
Marci Axelbank
Carl Babbitt
Charles Bartlett
Barry Bellows
Bruce Bellows
Harold Binder
MaryLou Blaine
Charles Brady
Virginia Breshears
Michael Breshears
Bob Brown
Nicholas Brown
Tafi Brown
Ole Bye
Judy Checchi
Don Clark
David Collins
Chris Covel
David Crosby
Joanna Dennett
Carol Drummond
Dale Dustin
The Eagle Times
Stacy Eaton
Eleanor Elbers
Steve Fortier
Hazel Fuller

John Fuller
Margaret Gacek
Paul Garcia
Heather Gendron
David Germain
Dale Guinn
Kurt Hackler
Dan Hall
Minnie Haskins
Patty Hatch
Wayne Hatch
Cindy Heath
Erin Heidorn
Michael Heidorn
Heidi Helmut
Cindy Hendrick
Heidi Hernes
David Hogan
Julie Hogan
Steve Hooper
Karyn Kaminski
The Keene Sentinel
Kitty Kmiec
Jan Kobeski
Cassandra Kreek
Ray L'Abbe
Bob LaPree
Evan Maltby
Roger Maltby

Wesley Marple
Jeff Marsden
Paul Massicotte
Monadock United Way
David W. Moody
Jeanne Moody
Michael Moore
Kate Tarlow Morgan
Cindi A. Nadelman
New Hampshire Dam Bureau
New Hampshire Department of Environmental Services
New Hampshire Department of Safety
New Hampshire Geological Survey
New Hampshire Office of Emergency Planning
New Hampshire State Police
New Hampshire Union Leader
Annette Newton
Barbara Noll
Margaret Chase Perry
Nathan Perry
Karen Plaisted
Linda Putnam
Heidi Quinn
Betty Ramsey

Bobbi Ramsey
Darrah Ramsey
Haas Ramsey
Russell Ramsey
Randall Rhoades
Donalin Ring
The River Record
John Sheldon
Gregory B. Sherwood
Derek Snelling
Sherry Stanley
Walter Striedieck
Neil Swift
Joe Szuch
Kathy Torrey
Michelle VanAlstyne
Todd Walier
Ken Walsh
Erwin Ward
Fraser Whitbread
Susan Whitbread
Barbara "Bobbie" Wilson
Gene Wilson
Sarah Wilson
Elizabeth Winham
Michael Wright